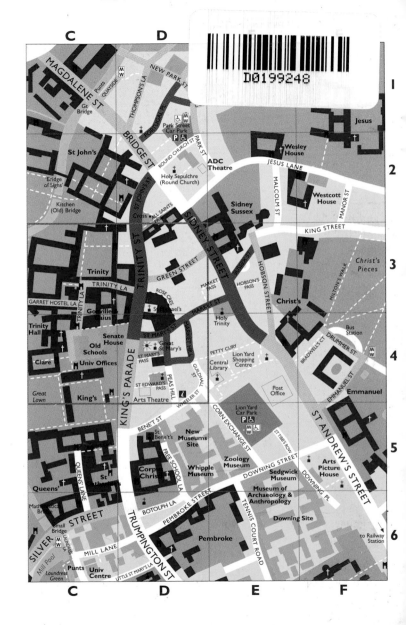

# CAMBRIDGE

...MORE THAN A GUIDE

JARROLD
publishing

# CAMBRIDGE

...MORE THAN A GUIDE

ANNIE BULLEN

**Acknowledgements**
Photography © Jarrold
Publishing by Neil
Jinkerson.
Additional photography
by kind permission of:
Bridgeman Art Library;
Annie Bullen; Cambridge
& County Folk Museum;
John Curtis; John
Heseltine; Sandra Ireland;
Kettle's Yard; Scott Polar
Research Institute.

The publishers wish to
thank Lena Pledger for
her invaluable assistance;
also the many Cambridge
businesses for their
kindness in allowing
us to photograph their
premises.

Printed in Singapore.
ISBN 0 7117 2953 0  1/04

Designer:
Simon Borrough
Editor:
Angela Royston
Artwork and walk maps:
Clive Goodyer
City maps:
The Map Studio, Romsey,
Hants. Main map based
on cartography ©
George Phillip Ltd

Front cover: Bicycles in
Cambridge

Previous page:
Peterhouse College

# CONTENTS

St John's College

WELCOME
TO CAMBRIDGE

Cambridge is a city of contradictions. Ancient it certainly is – the evidence of old stone-work, antique carvings, lofty statues and narrow, twisting dark passageways lies before you at every turn of the road.

This great heritage has not stifled the city, however. Scientists and thinkers have thrived over the centuries in its spacious courts, its gardens and in its university. In the late 17th century Isaac Newton discovered the laws of motion and laid the foundations for modern physics, and nearly 100 years later Charles Darwin returned to Cambridge after his voyage in the *Beagle* to write *The Origin of Species*. Charles Babbage built the first computer, Ernest Rutherford and his team split the atom, the jet engine was developed here by Frank Whittle, and the secret of life itself, neatly encoded into the double helix that is DNA, was untangled by Cambridge scientists.

Come to Cambridge today and you won't be bored by its antiquity or overawed by its cleverness. You will fall in love with the beauty of the city encircled by its river, the lively feel of the streets, the independence of the businesses and the easiness of access to the heart of the city – its university. Most of the 31 colleges welcome visitors and you can spend happy hours marvelling at their ancient beauty. Use this guide to enjoy a wonderful city that offers as much to the 21st-century visitor as it has done over the years to the many thousands of creative people who have called it home.

Trinity College

# HIGHLIGHTS

Where do you start in Cambridge among the ancient streets with their twisting passageways and colleges? The arresting view of King's College and its chapel is a magnet for many people. Glimpses of the busy marketplace and punts drifting by on the river are also enticing, so it's worth picking out some of the highlights to begin with. There's lots more to follow.

View from Great St Mary's

## START AT THE TOP

You'll get a bird's-eye view of the city if you can brave the 123 steps of the tower of Great St Mary's in St Mary's Passage (map D4). This is the principal church in Cambridge, used for both university and civic occasions. There's a small charge for climbing the tower, which has a tremendous peal of 12 bells, all in working order.

**Open:** daily 8.00–20.00 (tower)
**Entry to tower**: under £5
**Further information:** page 40

## KING'S COLLEGE CHAPEL
### King's Parade; map C4

Most of us have watched and listened to the Festival of Nine Lessons and Carols broadcast each Christmas from King's College Chapel. The music is moving and the chapel looks tremendous even on television, but nothing can prepare you for the real thing. Look for Rubens' tender painting, *The Adoration of the Magi*, above the altar and admire the carved wooden choir stalls. After visiting the chapel walk behind it towards Scholar's Piece. As you turn back you'll see the famous view beloved of photographers and illustrators.

Evensong is sung daily during term, except for Mondays, and you are very welcome to attend. You can sit in those famous choir stalls to listen to one of the best choirs in the country.

**Open:** daily – check boards outside the main gate for times
**Entry:** under £5
**Further information:** pages 42–43

SMOKE-FREE ZONE

Services in the great King's College Chapel are performed by candlelight, giving a wonderful atmosphere, but, at one time, blackening the walls with smoke. Since the chapel was cleaned and altered in the 1960s to take Rubens' great painting *The Adoration of the Magi*, special smokeless candles from Sweden have been used.

King's College Chapel

## ENJOY THE ART

Two world-renowned galleries lie
at opposite ends of Cambridge, and
they couldn't be more different. The
Fitzwilliam Museum in Trumpington
Street is a grand and beautiful building.
It holds not only a terrific collection of
paintings, drawings and prints but also
textiles, silver, ceramics and much more.
Allow plenty of time for your visit.

Kettle's Yard (map B1) is the strange
name for the group of cottages and
gallery extension that houses what was
once an extraordinary private collection
of 20th-century paintings, pots and
sculpture. It belonged to one-time Tate
Gallery curator Jim Ede who lived here
for many years before giving the whole
collection to the university. It is strangely
moving to see the paintings hung exactly
as they would have been when he and
his wife, Helen, lived here.

**Open:** Fitzwilliam Museum: Tue–Sat
10.00–17.00; Sun and bank holiday Mon
12.00–17.00. Closed until June 2004 for
refurbishment (check website for re-
opening date)
Kettle's Yard: Tue–Sun and bank holiday
Mon; mid-Apr–mid-Aug: 13.30–16.30;
mid-Aug–mid-Apr: 14.00–16.00
**Entry:** free to both
**Further information:**
Fitzwilliam Museum pages 38–39
Kettle's Yard pages 41–42

## BOTANIC GARDEN

Don't be put off by the word 'botanic'.
The 16-hectare (40-acre) Botanic
Garden in Bateman Street can be
enjoyed by everyone, plant-lover or not.

Kettle's Yard

If you like to walk, it is a pleasant stroll
down Trumpington Street to reach the
gardens, where you'll find a lake, woodland area, a rock garden, systematic
beds showing plants growing with other
members of the same family, lawns,
streams, glasshouses full of exotic specimens and even a grass maze for children
to explore. You can bring your own
picnic or buy a snack and something to
drink at the café.

**Open:** daily from 10.00; closing times
vary with the season (ring to check).
Closed over the Christmas period
(please check before visiting)
**Entry:** Mar–end Oct: under £5;
Nov–end Feb: free on weekdays, under
£5 on weekends and bank holidays
**Further information:** page 34

## TREAT YOURSELF

Choose a lovely sunny day and book a punt (see page 83) complete with strawberries and cream and a large jug of Pimms. Take your time travelling lazily along the river or find a peaceful spot to tie up and enjoy the experience. Decadent or what?

Botanic Garden

## SECRET GARDENS

Of course you'll want to explore some of the colleges (see pages 32–55 for details) but what many visitors don't realize is the beauty of their gardens. The thick walls of Gonville and Caius muffle the traffic and, once inside the gardens, all you hear is bird song. Clare College has particularly lovely gardens with a tranquil pond set in a sunken lawn, clipped hedges and wonderfully planted herbaceous borders. See if you can spot the missing bit on Clare Bridge (see page 36). Emmanuel College has not one but three very lovely gardens. Everyone wants to see the Fellows' Garden here but they keep it mainly to themselves, opening only occasionally for charity. When you visit St John's you'll admire the famous Bridge of Sighs but don't miss a stroll around the grounds to admire the grand view of sweeping lawns, well-stocked flower beds and the gently flowing river. Christ's College is another for garden lovers to enjoy – there's the added pleasure here of a row of beehives for the Fellows' honey, a swimming bath and a mulberry tree said to have been planted the year Milton was born – 1608.

**Open:** opening times and entry fees vary – see main entry for each of these colleges on pages 32–55

St John's College garden

## SCIENTIFIC DISCOVERY

Cambridge is renowned for its great scientists and the facilities that enabled them to make their discoveries. In the 17th century William Harvey, a Cambridge man, discovered how blood circulates in the body and Isaac Newton studied at Trinity. In the mid-19th century Charles Darwin was a pupil of Adam Sedgwick. In 1953 Francis Crick and James Watson discovered DNA at the university's Cavendish Laboratory. They called a press conference to announce their discovery at the lab's favourite pub – the Eagle in Bene't Street (see page 78). There's a blue plaque on the wall to that effect. Today you might see the brilliant Professor Stephen Hawking, who wrote *A Brief History of Time*, beetling around the city in his wheelchair.

Many of the university labs and scientific teaching resources have museums attached that are open to the public. There's the Scott Polar Research Institute in Lensfield Road off Trumpington Street, the Sedgwick Museum of Earth Sciences in Downing Street (map E5), the Whipple Museum of the History of Science in Free School Lane (map D5) and the Museum of Archaeology and Anthropology in Downing Street (map E5).
**Open:** see individual entries (pages 33–55)
**Entry:** free to each museum
**Further information:** pages 32–55

## LITERARY JOURNEY

There are many specialist bookshops in Cambridge and if you've been after a particular volume for ages, the chances are that you'll find it here. The Haunted Bookshop in St Edward's Passage (map D4) sells secondhand children's books and illustrated editions while, just round the corner, G. David will keep you happily browsing all day. Heffers is in Trinity Street (map D3) while some say the Oxfam Bookshop in Sidney Street (map E3) is the place to go.

Take time to see the celebrated Pepys Library at Magdalene College where the 3,000 books left by the diarist are arranged from 1 to 3,000 – by size. Samuel Pepys, who was at Magdalene from 1651–54, insisted that his collection, which includes his six volumes of diaries, should remain entire.
**Open:** daily; early Oct–mid-Mar 14.30–15.30; late April–end Aug 11.30–12.30, 14.30–15.30
**Further information:** page 44

### STRANGERS AND BROTHERS

This series of novels, detailing the fictional life of barrister Lewis Elliot, was written by chemist and physicist C.P. Snow (Charles Percy Snow aka Baron Snow of Leicester). Snow, who studied at Christ's College, wrote the series, which includes such favourites as *The Masters*, *The Corridors of Power*, *Time of Hope* and *The Affair*, over a period of 30 years. Much of the action takes place in Cambridge during a time when important scientific breakthroughs were being made.

**TREAT YOURSELF**
Revisit the books of your childhood with a trip to the Haunted Bookshop in St Edward's Passage (map D4) where you'll find them all from *Swallows and Amazons* to Jennings, from *Just William* to Biggles. And if you enjoyed comics such as *The Eagle* or *Bunty*, there's a good chance you'll find the annual versions here.

## GO PUBBING ...

On sunny days you'll probably head for the river – walk down Silver Street or Mill Lane (map C6) for a seat outside The Anchor, where you have a ringside view of people and their punts. The nearby Mill will let you take your drink across the lane to Laundress Green where you can sit and watch the water. Another favourite is The Eagle in Bene't Street (map D5) with its carefully preserved ceiling bearing the smoky signatures of dozens of young airmen. If you want something quieter, make for the Cambridge Blue in Gwydir Street, the Free Press in Prospect Row or the strangely named Champion of the Thames in King Street (map F3).
**Further information:** pages 77–78

## OR PUNTING ...

Everyone thinks they can zoom stylishly down the river with a casual push of the pole – but it's not so easy. Don't be put off though – not too many people fall in and the river is very shallow.
**Further information:** pages 17–18

The Anchor pub

The Backs

## ... OR BOTH

Combine pubbing and punting and make your way up the river to pretty Grantchester, once home to poet Rupert Brooke and now the more notorious Lord Archer. You leave from the Mill Lane punting station (map C6). It will take you up to two hours to negotiate the 4 km (2.5 miles) of river, but there are several good pubs and a pretty tea garden to revive you and stoke you up for the return journey. Alternatively you can ask the punting company to provide a hamper for a picnic or barbeque on the riverbank.

**Further information:** page 83

St John's College

# PLEASURES AND PERILS OF PUNTING

Punting on the Cam

One hundred years ago when the River Cam was crowded, smelly, dirty and noisy because it was full of barges and boats, no one would have dreamed of taking a punt out for pleasure. Now that our roads are crowded, smelly, dirty and noisy and the river is comparatively clean, everyone does – at least it seems that way in Cambridge. And why not, when you can sit back and enjoy some of the loveliest riverside views in England, as you drift slowly along?

Punts were originally working boats, designed without a keel so that they could be manoeuvred through the fens by wildfowlers or reed-cutters. Now students and tourists alike enjoy the pleasures and suffer the humiliations of punting. Many of the colleges have their own punts in college colours and with improbable names, hired to members at a fraction of the cost of the tourist boats, which is why some students become adept at the not-so-easy art of poling their way up the river.

boat at the back. This is considered bad form in Cambridge and something you should never do. Don't hurry as you lift the pole completely clear of the water before letting it slip vertically back in, close to the side of the punt, until you touch the riverbed. With the pole angled very slightly forwards, grip it tightly and push downwards, moving your hands along its length as you keep pushing. As the punt moves forward and you start to 'run out' of pole, twist it slightly to release it and let it float up. As it does so, use it as

Clare College from the Backs

**AND IS THERE HONEY?**

Just a couple of miles – easy punting distance – from the city centre is the pretty village of Grantchester, home to poet Rupert Brooke and very much on his mind as he sent poems back to England on his way to war in 1914/15. The church clock is no longer stuck at 'ten to three' but you will be able to find 'honey still for tea' if you go there.

It's common to feel – as you balance uneasily on that flat board for the first time, letting the heavy wooden pole slip through your hands – that you have suddenly become the focus of everyone's attention. You have, but take no notice. Hardly anyone else knows how to do it properly either.

Most of the punts in Cambridge now have flat platforms at both ends, so there's no doubt where you should stand. In Oxford they stand inside the

a rudder to steer, before starting the drop-and-push operation all over again.

It's not quite as easy as it sounds, especially when you can see all those non-punters leaning over the nearest bridge hoping to see you make a big splash. But the sense of achievement when you finally get the hang of it makes it all worthwhile. It's not necessary to wear a boater and neckerchief (men) or a floaty dress and hat (women), but a jug of Pimms might be nice (see page 83).

Clare Bridge

# PLANNING YOUR VISIT

Magdalene College

Ancient and modern is probably a good way to sum up Cambridge. Perhaps because the city is largely traffic-free, you get a good feel for the past. Winding passageways connect the streets. The medieval college walls, enormous wooden gateways, old stone sculptures and statues are on all sides as you walk through the city.

But Cambridge, more than any other university city, has embraced science and scientific research whole-heartedly. Perhaps that's why the city has a lively buzz. Here are a few suggestions to help you make the most of your time in Cambridge, whether you are there for a few hours only, or two or three days.

## DAY ONE

King's College Chapel is set back from King's Parade, where the road widens. This area was the centre of the medieval town – a clutter of wharves, houses and mills – but the college's founder,

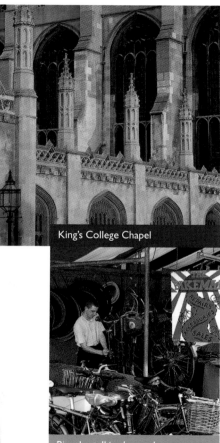

King's College Chapel

Bicycle stall in the market

Henry VI, demolished the lot in 1446 to make space for an imposing new chapel. King's College Chapel (see page 42) is the most grand and beautiful building in Cambridge and the most visited. Don't let that put you off. The late Gothic chapel is spacious and full of history and fine craftsmanship. No fewer than five English monarchs came and went before the chapel was completed, and there was input from Henry VII (with a nudge from his mother Lady Margaret Beaufort who herself founded Christ's and St John's colleges) and Henry VIII. Allow at least an hour for a good look before exploring the courts and grounds of King's College itself.

Time for coffee now. You could just pop across the road to Auntie's (see page 71) or make your way to the tiny entrance of St Edward's Passage (map D4) opposite where, as you wind your way around, you'll find the Indigo Coffee House and O'Brien's. Take time to visit one or both of the bookshops in this little lane. You might like to explore St Edward's Church too – its proper name is St Edward King and Martyr and it is dedicated to the Saxon King Edward, murdered in 978 at the tender age of 15 at Corfe Castle by his stepmother.

Follow St Edward's Passage round into Peas Hill and on to the marketplace where you might like a browse among the many and varied stalls. If you want a quick way to get your bearings, visit the nearby Tourist Information Centre in Wheeler Street (map D4) to ask about the closest boarding point for an open-top bus sightseeing trip. If a pub lunch appeals, the Eagle in Bene't Street (map D5) isn't too far away. If it's a sunny day you might prefer to sit outside at The Anchor in Silver Street (map C6). Get there early though – others will have the same idea. You can also eat outside at La Mimosa in Rose Crescent (map D3) which opens into the marketplace.

**Round Church**

After lunch stroll up to Magdalene Street (map C1). On the way you'll see a perfectly round church. This is the oldest of the four remaining circular churches in Britain and is properly called the Church of the Holy Sepulchre (map D2). After your visit, carry on along Bridge Street and into Magdalene Street, old with some lovely shops. At the end of the street you'll spot Kettle's Yard (see page 41) just across the road. This extraordinary 'art gallery' is open only in the after-

noons (not on Mondays though). Make your way to the house first, and ring the bell to be admitted.

If you've got the energy afterwards, walk back into town, down Trumpington Street (map D6) to the famous bakery, Fitzbillies (see page 73), where they'll do you a nice cup of tea and a plate of their famous Chelsea buns.

An uplifting way to end the first day's visit to Cambridge is to attend Evensong in one of the college chapels. Look on the boards outside King's or St John's to see the times.

## DAYS TWO AND THREE

Here are some suggestions to choose from to add to what you've already seen and done.

**Trinity College**

Trinity College

Clare College garden

## Visit the colleges

Look at the boards outside the main gates for opening times and entry fees, if there are any. The colleges backing on to the river such as St John's and Clare are special, in that you have views of the water. Some of the colleges have particularly lovely gardens – Clare, Emmanuel and Trinity are all worth visiting. Generally you'll see the courts (the rectangular square areas, called 'quads' in Oxford), around which the buildings are arranged, the chapel, sometimes the dining hall and library. But please go only where you're directed and walk quietly – someone is bound to be working.

## Be a punter

Even if you don't want to do it yourself you can hire a 'chauffeur' with your punt. The person wielding the pole will give you a lot of interesting information as you go. See page 83 for details of punting stations.

## Cambridge on foot

For a fascinating insight into the history and architecture of Cambridge, join one of the daily guided walks round the city led by a Blue Badge guide (see page 83), or you can follow one of the 'go-it-alone' walks on pages 26–31.

## Picnic in the park

Put together the ingredients for a picnic – try the Cambridge Cheese Company in All Saints Passage (map D2), or buy it ready made from Peppercorns in either Rose Crescent (map D3) or King's Parade (map D4) – and find a sunny riverbank where you can sit and watch the world and punts go by. See pages 56–57 for the best open spaces and gardens where you can picnic.

Reiss, Trinity Street (page 64)

## Retail therapy

Shops away from your own home town are much more interesting and never more so than in Cambridge. The shopping guide (pages 58–69) gives the areas where you'll find independent retailers, or try the shopping walk on page 28. The big High-Street names are in Lion Yard (map E4), Sidney Street (map D2–E4) and the Grafton Centre, off King Street.

## Art and science

All the excellent university museums in Cambridge give you free entry. Full details of these are found on pages 32–55. If you prefer the arts, go to the Fitzwilliam Museum in Trumpington Street to see its world-class collections of paintings, ceramics, antiquities, textiles, glass, silver, furniture and more besides. Or try the Museum of Classical

Archaeology in Sidgwick Avenue (map A6) or the Museum of Archaeology and Anthropology in Downing Street (map E5). Scientists and historians will enjoy the Scott Polar Institute in Lensfield Road, the Sedgwick Museum of Earth Sciences in Downing Street (map E5) or the Whipple Museum of the History of Science in Free School Lane (map D5). Everyone will love the Museum of Zoology in Downing Street (map E5).

Peppercorns

Botanic Garden

## WHO IS IT?

It might be fanciful to imagine that one of the statues flanking the door of the chapel in Corpus Christi College has a large nose and an enquiring expression. But both those features have been attributed to Matthew Parker, Master of Corpus Christi in 1544 and later Archbishop of Canterbury. His perpetual questioning and over-sized nose gave him the nickname 'Nosey Parker' – a term that is still used today.

### Smell the flowers

It is just 1.5 km (under a mile) along Trumpington Street to the 16-hectare (40-acre) Botanic Garden which has a lot to keep plant lovers happy. Walk out there in the morning and stop at the excellent Brown's on the way back for a slap-up lunch. You've earned it.

# WALKS

There are excellent daily guided walks starting from the Tourist Information Centre (TIC) in Wheeler Street (see page 94), but here are three suggestions if you'd like to go it alone.

## BRIDGES AND ALLEYWAYS WALK

As you would expect in a city encircled by a river, there are plenty of historic bridges. This walk takes you across some of them and explores a few intriguing lanes.

Start at Magdalene – pronounced 'maudlin' – Bridge (Great Bridge). The first bridge, a wooden affair, was built nearly 1,200 years ago. This one was built in 1823. Walk down Bridge Street, stopping to explore Portugal Place, a pretty street on your left. It is named for the quantities of port once shipped to Cambridge to add to the pleasures of college High Tables.

Back to Bridge Street and a pause at the Round Church before turning right down St John's Street. If St John's College

is open, go in and make your way through the courts to Kitchen Bridge where you stand to look at the Bridge of Sighs (nothing like its famous namesake) linking New Court to the old part of the college.

Leave St John's by the main gate, turning right along Trinity Street until you pass Caius College when you turn right down Senate House Passage. Notice the Gate of Honour with its double-faced sundial. Bear left to Clare College. Go in, walking through the college to Clare Bridge and the beautiful gardens. Cross Clare Bridge and turn left through the gardens to follow the Backs past Queens' College to Silver Street. Turn left and to your left is the wooden Mathematical Bridge, joining Queens' buildings. Turn right into Laundress

Lane; carry on down Granta Place past the University Centre and turn left into Little St Mary's Lane. The half moon on the wall of an old cottage is an old inn sign. Turn left at the end and cross the road to walk up Pembroke Street, soon turning left into Free School Lane, where the famous Cavendish Laboratories once stood.

Turn right at Bene't Street and left and left again

Magdalene College

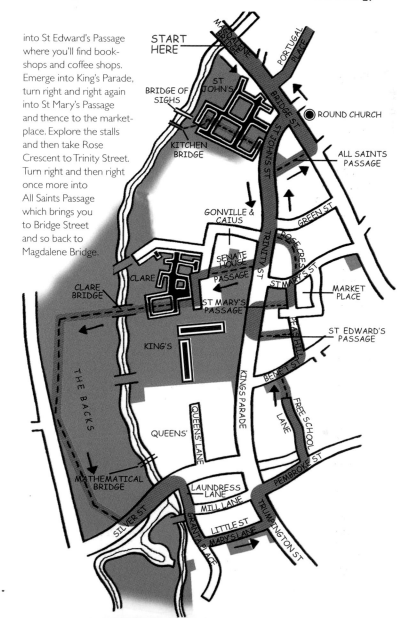

into St Edward's Passage where you'll find book-shops and coffee shops. Emerge into King's Parade, turn right and right again into St Mary's Passage and thence to the market-place. Explore the stalls and then take Rose Crescent to Trinity Street. Turn right and then right once more into All Saints Passage which brings you to Bridge Street and so back to Magdalene Bridge.

START HERE

ST JOHN'S

BRIDGE OF SIGHS

PORTUGAL PLACE

ROUND CHURCH

BRIDGE ST

KITCHEN BRIDGE

ST JOHN'S ST

ALL SAINTS PASSAGE

GONVILLE & CAIUS

GREEN ST

TRINITY ST

ROSE CRES

CLARE BRIDGE

SENATE HOUSE

PASSAGE

ST MARY'S ST

MARKET PLACE

CLARE

ST MARY'S PASSAGE

PEAS HILL

ST EDWARD'S PASSAGE

THE BACKS

KING'S

KINGS PARADE

BENET ST

FREE SCHOOL LANE

QUEENS LANE

QUEENS'

LAUNDRESS LANE

MILL LANE

PEMBROKE ST

MATHEMATICAL BRIDGE

SILVER ST

GRANTA PLACE

LITTLE ST MARY'S LANE

TRUMPINGTON ST

## STOPPING TO SHOP WALK

Cambridge has some excellent shopping streets and is also full of interesting individually-owned shops (see pages 58–69). This walk will lead you past some of them – whether you choose to do more than window shop is up to you. This walk could take some time – but there are plenty of cafés on the way.

and walk past the TIC in Wheeler Street to reach Bene't Street. Browse through the shops before turning right into King's Parade. Walk along this grand street with its lovely shops and splendid King's College on your left. But first divert along St Edward's Passage on the right – there are two good bookshops here – before returning to King's Parade.

Start in the marketplace where you might find some stalls you didn't expect. Leave by Guildhall Street

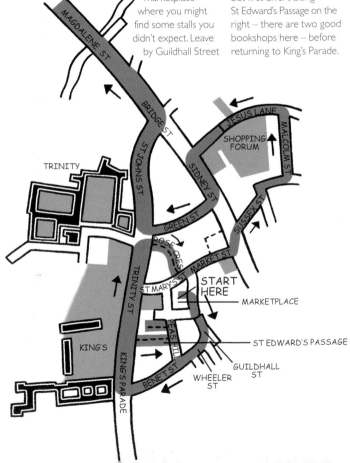

MAGDALENE ST

BRIDGE ST

ST JOHNS ST

TRINITY

SIDNEY ST

JESUS LANE

SHOPPING FORUM

MALCOLM ST

GREEN ST

SUSSEX ST

ROSE CRES

TRINITY ST

ST MARYS ST

MARKET ST

START HERE — MARKETPLACE

KING'S

KING'S PARADE

PEAS HILL

ST EDWARD'S PASSAGE

BENE'T ST

WHEELER ST

GUILDHALL ST

Keep walking as King's Parade turns into Trinity Street where there are plenty more tempting windows. When you've exhausted Trinity Street go along Rose Crescent.

Walk up this curving pedestrian street, with shops selling cosmetics, gifts, fashionable leather goods and toys. At the end you'll find yourself facing the marketplace. Turn left and follow Market Street to Sidney Street. Cross the road into

**TREAT YOURSELF**

You don't need a way-out handbag or an outrageously different, but gorgeous, pair of shoes – but most women really would like to own them. Just walk down Green Street and you'll find shops full of things that definitely come into the 'treat' category.

Sussex Street where there's a cluster of good shops. Carry on to your left, turning left down Malcolm Street and left again down Jesus Lane until you reach the newish Shopping Forum with

Primavera (page 67)

several good outlets. Walk back towards the city centre, turning left again into Sidney Street and head for Green Street on your right, with lots of original boutiques and shoe shops.

You emerge opposite Trinity College. Turn right here and follow the curve of St John's Street, turning left into Bridge Street. Keep going across the bridge to Magdalene Street with its lovely old buildings housing some very good shops, cafés and restaurants.

Rose Crescent

## PEOPLE AND PLACES WALK

So many people who have left their mark on the world were nurtured in Cambridge. This walk, ending at Trinity College, shows where some of them lived and worked. Start in Bene't Street outside The Eagle pub. Here is a blue plaque, unveiled in 2003 by James Watson, one of the scientists who discovered the double helix structure of DNA, the so-called 'secret of life'. Watson worked with Francis Crick at the world-famous Cavendish Laboratory, then down Free School Lane. He, Crick and Maurice Wilkins received a Nobel Prize in 1962. Sadly the other scientist responsible for the discovery, Rosalind Franklin, who was a Newnham College graduate, was not named on the

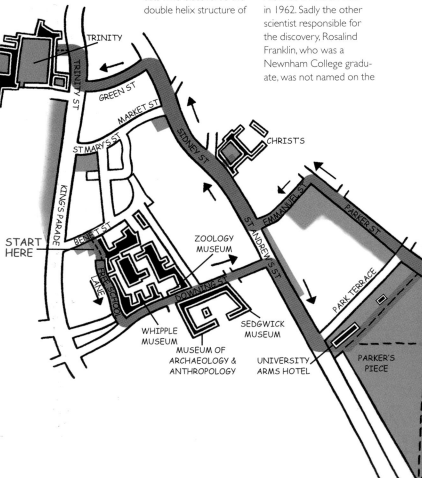

TRINITY

TRINITY ST

GREEN ST

MARKET ST

ST MARY'S ST

SIDNEY ST

CHRIST'S

KING'S PARADE

BENE'T ST

ST ANDREW'S ST

EMMANUEL ST

PARKER ST

START HERE

FREE SCHOOL LANE

ZOOLOGY MUSEUM

DOWNING ST

PARK TERRACE

WHIPPLE MUSEUM

SEDGWICK MUSEUM

MUSEUM OF ARCHAEOLOGY & ANTHROPOLOGY

UNIVERSITY ARMS HOTEL

PARKER'S PIECE

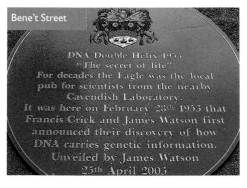

Bene't Street

DNA Double Helix 1953
"The secret of life"
For decades the Eagle was the local
pub for scientists from the nearby
Cavendish Laboratory.
It was here on February 28th 1953 that
Francis Crick and James Watson first
announced their discovery of how
DNA carries genetic information.
Unveiled by James Watson
25th April 2003

Nobel citation – she died tragically young in 1958. Walk down Free School Lane. The Cavendish Laboratory, where Ernest Rutherford worked on the structure of the atom and where Crockcroft and Walton split it, used to be here, before moving to a new campus in 1974. But if you turn left into Downing Street, you'll find a cluster of university museums with many associations. Charles Darwin, a Christ's College graduate, upset his old mentor, Professor Sedgwick with his theory of evolution. You'll see many specimens sent back from Darwin's voyage of discovery in the Zoology Museum. Across the road is the Sedgwick Museum, named after the distinguished geologist.

Jack Hobbs was an English cricketing legend in the 1920s. The eldest of 12 from a poor family, John Berry Hobbs learned his craft in Cambridge. Walk to the end of Downing Street, turning right at St Andrew's Street until you come to Parker's Piece. Go on to the green, past the University Arms Hotel and you'll come to the Hobbs Pavilion, opened by the great man himself in 1930 and now a restaurant. His photograph and achievements cover a wall.

From cricket to poetry. Walk across the rest of the green to Parker Street, turn left and left again into Emmanuel Street and right into St Andrew's Street and walk along to the great gate of Christ's. John Milton, who wrote *Paradise Lost*, studied at Christ's College for several years from 1628. Go in if the college is open. Milton's rooms were in the left-hand corner of the first court. If the Fellows' Garden is open, you'll see the ancient mulberry tree underneath which Milton allegedly sat and wrote poetry.

Leave Christ's by the main gate and turn down Sidney Street and Green Street to emerge opposite Trinity College. On the right of the gate by the chapel you'll see another tree – said to be a descendant of the apple tree whose falling fruit supposedly triggered Isaac Newton's understanding that gravity also governs the movement of heavenly bodies. You can see Newton's statue along with those of other Trinity men, Francis Bacon and Alfred, Lord Tennyson in the ante-chapel. The poet Lord Byron's statue is in the Wren Library.

Sir Isaac Newton, Trinity College

# SIGHTSEEING

Of course you'll want to see the colleges with their beautifully maintained courts, lawns and gardens, historic chapels and wonderful riverside walks. But Cambridge has even more to offer – world-class museums (most of them free), galleries and unique churches.

Most of the city centre is pedestrianized during the day, but watch out for the silent and ubiquitous bicycle. College opening times vary – some still close from mid-April until mid-June while exams are taking place. Events also affect opening times, which are displayed daily on boards outside the main gates. Please remember to observe notices asking you to visit quietly and not to walk on the grass. Disabled access is often restricted because of the nature of the ancient buildings – the porter on the gate will be happy to tell you what you can see.

## The Backs
### map B2–B6

Once known as the 'Backsides' these are areas of riverbank, garden, grassy meadow and pathway behind the six riverside colleges. Each piece of the Backs is owned separately by the college it adjoins, which gives an attractive mix of landscape. You can punt along the river or walk along the footpath.

The Backs

### WATER FIGHT

It was in 1829 that the best rowers from each of the two great universities, Cambridge and Oxford, battled it out in the first University Boat Race. Cambridge issued that initial challenge but Oxford, rowing nearer home at Henley-on-Thames, won.

## Botanic Garden
Bateman Street

This is a place for enjoyment just as much as for learning. Less than a mile from the city centre, the garden can be reached on foot. If you're not feeling up to a walk, use the Trumpington Road Park and Ride bus (see page 95) and get off at the Bateman Street stop.

Cambridge is a city with a lot of green space and the Botanic Garden gives you that – with around 8,000 different species of plants, arranged in areas best suited to their needs. There are stream and bog gardens for those species that like to have their toes in the water and a dry garden for plants that don't. British wild plants have space too – with areas for arable weeds, chalk-loving alpines and plants that thrive in the fens. The systematic beds, organizing plants into their families, are arranged beautifully and labelled so that you can see what is related to what, while the herbaceous beds will take your breath away. Children will love exploring the grass maze and you are welcome to bring picnics. On weekdays you can enter from Bateman Street and Station Road, but at weekends and on bank holidays entry is from Bateman Street only.

### DON'T MISS
The glasshouses stuffed full of exotic species, alpines and gorgeous, showy tropical plants.
The lake, the woodland garden, the rose garden, the year-round autumn garden and the typical old-fashioned Cambridgeshire hedgerow.

**Open:** daily from 10.00; closing times vary with the season (ring to check). Closed over the Christmas period (check before visiting)
**Entry:** Mar–end Oct: under £5; Nov–end Feb: free on weekdays, under £5 on weekends and bank holidays
**Tel:** 01223 336265
**Website:** www.botanic.cam.ac.uk
**Disabled access:** full – disabled visitors and one companion admitted free
**Other facilities:** café, open daily (except weekdays Nov–end Feb); shop, open Mar–end Oct; picnic area

Botanic Garden

## Cambridge and County Folk Museum
### Castle Street; map C1

In 1935 local people, concerned that evidence of a rapidly changing way of life was fast disappearing, devoted time and energy to getting this museum established. Since then around 30,000 objects, each connected with the way of life in Cambridgeshire, have been collected, listed and displayed. Home life, craft and trade, university, toys and games and local pubs are all explained. The building itself, originally a farmhouse and for many years a pub – the White Horse Inn – is old and timber framed, with winding stairways and small rooms, each full of displays. Florence Ada Keynes, one of the first female undergraduates at Newnham, helped run the museum until her death in 1958 at the age of 96, while Enid Porter, curator for nearly 30 years, is the author of the standard book on Cambridgeshire customs and folklore.

Today the museum not only explains how life was in the county, but also runs workshops, educational activities for children and adult education courses.
**Open:** Apr–Sep: Mon–Sat 10.30–17.00, Sun 14.00–17.00; Oct–Mar: Tue–Sat 10.30–17.00, Sun 14.00–17.00 (open Mon during school holidays). Closed 24 Dec–1 Jan; closed until summer 2004 (ring to check re-opening date)
**Entry:** under £5
**Tel:** 01223 355159
**Website:** www.folkmuseum.org.uk
**Disabled access:** full
**Other facilities:** shop

## Cambridge Brass Rubbing Centre

Cambridge Brass Rubbing Centre, run by the knowledgeable and enthusiastic Kristin Randall, has no permanent home for the time being. But you can see the brasses, hear their history and make some rubbings to take home by telephoning Kristin who will give you directions to the

Cambridge and County Folk Museum

venue she is using. She'll entertain you with facts about the figures that appear on the brasses (such as the bears, lions, dragons and dogs used as footrests) and may even put on her 14th-century helmet and sword to inspire you.

**Entry:** there is a charge for making a brass rubbing

**Tel:** 01223 871621

Christ's College gateway

## Christ's College
### St Andrew's Street; map E4

Wander round the courts and enjoy the gardens – you'll notice a sharp contrast between the original old courts and the dramatically modern one designed by Sir Denys Lasdun in 1966. Don't miss the famous Fellows' Garden with its beehives, swimming bath and ancient mulberry tree. If you've visited St John's College you may recognize the beasts on the gate – they're the mythical yales of Lady Margaret Beaufort, the college's founder. The statue above the gate shows her, Bible in hand.

**Open:** daily 9.30–12.00 during vacation, 9.30–16.00 in term time; closed most of May and June (during exams)

**Entry:** free

**Tel:** 01223 334900

**Website:** www.christs.cam.ac.uk

## Clare College
### Trinity Lane; map C4

Clare, founded in 1326, is the second oldest college (Peterhouse is senior) although the elegant palace-like court was rebuilt in 1719. The gardens here are among the loveliest in Cambridge, featuring a pond in a sunken lawn, herbaceous borders – beautiful at any season – and a general air of tranquillity and unity.

Clare Bridge, framed by delicate wrought-iron gates, is decorated with 13 perfectly round stone balls – and one with a wedge taken out of it. True or not, the story goes that architect Thomas Grumbold was so unhappy with the paltry sum he was paid that he determined the bridge would never be complete. Despite that tiny flaw, it bears testimony to fine workmanship as it is the oldest surviving river bridge in the city.

**Open:** April–Oct daily 10.00–17.00

**Entry:** under £5

**Tel:** 01223 333200

**Website:** www.clare.cam.ac.uk

## Corpus Christi College
### Trumpington Street; map D5

You can enjoy walking round the two courts in this college, which was actually founded by the townspeople of

> **MARITIME MEMORIAL**
> Look for the memorial tablet to the great maritime explorer Captain James Cook in the sanctuary of the church of St Andrew the Great, opposite Christ's College, where one of his sons was an undergraduate.

Clare College

Cambridge in 1352. Old Court is generally reckoned to be the best surviving medieval court in the city. Although you can't go into the chapel, a glass panel allows you to peer inside. This is the college where the long-nosed, inquiring Matthew Parker (the original 'Nosey Parker') was Master in 1544. He later became Archbishop of Canterbury. His statue stands outside the chapel but the real tribute to him is the Parker Library (not open to the public) with its collection of rare books and manuscripts, many rescued by Parker after the dissolution of the monasteries.

**Open:** daily 14.00–16.00 except mid-April–mid-June (during exams)
**Entry:** free
**Tel:** 01223 338000
**Website:** www.corpus.cam.ac.uk

### Emmanuel College
St Andrew's Street; map F5

You can visit the hall and Wren's chapel here. Inside the latter is a plaque to John Harvard, a 17th-century undergraduate who sailed to the New World on the *Mayflower* and left money for his own foundation in America. It became

Corpus Christi Old Court

America's first and most famous university – Harvard. The three large gardens at Emmanuel are renowned for their beauty. The Fellows' Garden (very occasionally open) is home to a magnificent oriental plane tree.

**Open:** daily 9.00–18.00, limited visiting mid-May–mid-June (during exams). Closed at Christmas and Easter
**Entry:** free
**Tel:** 01223 334200
**Website:** www.emma.cam.ac.uk

### Fitzwilliam Museum
Trumpington Street
This is one of the world's great galleries and museums which, with the completion of the new courtyard development in mid-2004, has superb space to show its collection of paintings, drawings and

Emmanuel College          Harvard Window

On Chaldon Down

(check website for re-opening date)
**Entry:** free
**Tel:** 01223 332900
**Website:** www.fitzmuseum.cam.ac.uk
**Disabled access:** full
**Other facilities:** shop, café

**Gonville and Caius College**
Trinity Street; map D3
Do as the locals do and call this lovely
college 'Caius' – pronounced 'keys'
because one of the founders was John
Kees whose name was 'Latinized' to

prints. Recent acquisitions include an oil
painting by Samuel Palmer, *On Chaldon
Down*, Dorset, never shown before,
and red chalk drawings by Caravaggio.
You can also see glass, sculpture, silver,
textiles, many objects from ancient
Rome and Greece, clocks, ceramics, fans,
manuscripts and books. It is probably
better to make several visits rather than
attempt to see everything in one go.
**Open:** Tue–Sat 10.00–17.00; Sun and
bank holiday Mon 12.00–17.00. Closed
until June 2004 for refurbishment

**GATES OR GOALS?**
You'll see three magnificent
gates at Caius College. They
are symbols of stages that
students should pass through
in their academic life. First is
the Gate of Humility, to be
understood before the walk
through the Gate of Virtue.
The final stage is that great
day when, with head held
high, the student can march
through the Gate of Honour.

**LEADING BY
EXAMPLE**
America's first university was
founded by a one-time
Emmanuel undergraduate. John
Harvard studied at Cambridge in
the 1630s. He travelled across the
Atlantic, only to die of consump-
tion in New England. But he left
half his estate and more than 300
books to found a 'schoale', which
became Harvard University.

Caius. Walk inside and you'll think you're
in a secret garden – the thick walls
muffle the traffic noise and the bird-filled
gardens enclose you. Visit the chapel and
walk through the Gate of Humility and
the Gate of Virtue; these days the third
Gate, symbolizing Honour, is kept locked.
**Open:** daily 9.00–17.00 except
May–mid-June (during exams)
**Entry:** free
**Tel:** 01223 332400
**Website:** www.cai.cam.ac.uk

### Great St Mary's
St Mary's Passage; map D4

You'll rarely hear this, the principal church in Cambridge, called by its official title 'St Mary the Great'. It is regarded as the university church and the main city church. It is late Gothic, built between 1478 and 1519. Not many churches have a working peal of 12 bells but St Mary's does. A circle cut to the right of the west door of the tower is what is known as a 'datum point' – it marks the exact centre of the city and all distances to and from Cambridge are measured from here.

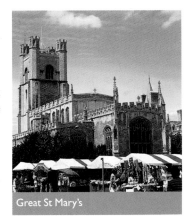

Great St Mary's

### DON'T MISS
A climb up the 123 steps to the top of the tower (which was added after the main body of the church was built) for a wonderful view over the city.

**Open:** daily, Mon–Sat 9.30–16.30, Sun 12.30–16.30
**Entry:** free (small charge for visiting tower)
**Tel:** 01223 741716
**Website:** www.ely.anglican.org/parishes/camgsm

The Gate of Honour, Gonville and Caius College

Jesus College

Kettle's Yard

### Jesus College
**Jesus Lane; map F2**

The chapel, the oldest college building in the city, contains a memorial to Thomas Cranmer, once an undergraduate and later Fellow here. Cranmer, the first Protestant Archbishop of Canterbury, was burned at the stake – in Oxford – for upholding his faith in Mary Tudor's Roman Catholic England. The chapel is the only building you can visit but the grounds are extensive and there's a pretty 16th-century cloister court.

**Open:** daily, dawn to dusk
**Entry:** free
**Tel:** 01223 339339
**Website:** www.jesus.cam.ac.uk

### Kettle's Yard
**Castle Street; map B1**

Every afternoon, except Mondays, you can climb the steps to what appears to be a tiny cottage, ring the bell, and ask to be admitted. A key will turn in the lock and you will enter the hallway of the most extraordinary collection of art you've ever visited. Kettle's Yard was the home of Jim Ede, once a curator at the Tate Gallery, London, and his wife, Helen.

Jim Ede's genius was in recognizing and encouraging great artistic talent. Over the years he bought or was given works by great painters and sculptors of the first half of the 20th century. He hung them on his walls (including the bathroom) or placed them on tables and shelves. Nothing is labelled or explained; you are free to wander round the house (and as you explore you'll see it's much much bigger than you first thought). Paintings by Ben and Winifred Nicholson, Alfred Wallis, Christopher Wood and David Jones – amongst others – hang on the walls.

### DON'T MISS
The attic room dedicated to the drawings of Henri Gaudier-Brzeska. There are his sculptures too and those of Henry

Moore, Barbara Hepworth and Brancusi.
Bowls by Lucie Rie, Bernard Leach and
Katherine Pleydell-Bouverie.
Books and arrangements of pebbles and
stones, left as the Edes enjoyed them.

Next door, the Kettle's Yard gallery has
changing exhibitions of contemporary
international art, supported by linked
events and talks. There's also music –
concerts in the house in spring and early
summer. Educational work includes clubs
and classes for children and lessons and
workshops for adults. Jim Ede died in
1990 but his house is still full of the spirit
of a man who believed that daily life
should embrace art and friends.

**Open:** house: Tue–Sun and bank holiday Mon; mid-Apr–mid-Aug:
13.30–16.30; mid-Aug–mid-Apr:
14.00–16.00
gallery: Tue–Sun and bank holiday Mon,
11.30–17.00
**Entry:** free
**Tel:** 01223 352124
**Website:** www.kettlesyard.co.uk
**Disabled access:** limited to house, full
to gallery
**Other facilities:** shop (in the gallery)

### King's College
King's Parade; map C4

If you are in Cambridge during term
time, it's well worth planning your visit
to include Evensong in King's College
Chapel. This wonderful late-Gothic building is known the world over for the
Christmas Eve Festival of Nine Lessons
and Carols, broadcast on radio and television. You can sit in those historic carved
wooden choir stalls, enjoy the singing of

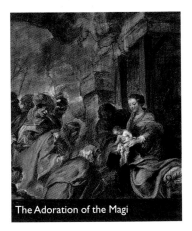
The Adoration of the Magi

one of the world's best choirs and look
at Rubens' tender *The Adoration of the
Magi* above the altar. When the painting
was given to the chapel in 1961, the
marble floor had to be lowered so
that the work could be hung without
obscuring the east window. A notice
outside the gate will tell you the time
of Evensong, which is sung daily except
on Mondays.

As you walk into the centre of
Cambridge, King's College and its chapel
is a focus for locals and tourists alike. The
long low wall outside the college, facing
King's Parade, is a favourite place to
meet, sit and watch the city go about its
business – people perch on the stone
like birds on telegraph wires. But walk
through the college gatehouse in the
middle of the carved stone screen and
you're in another world. A statue of the
college's founder, King Henry VI, can be
seen in the spacious Front Court. This

King's College Chapel ceiling

## DON'T MISS

The magnificent woodcarvings; look for the great oak screen separating the choir from the ante-chapel.

The initials 'H' and 'A' – Henry VIII and his second wife, Anne Boleyn – above the central doorway. Look too for a carved falcon from the Boleyn family arms and the initials 'RA' – Regina Anne.

*The Adoration of the Magi*, painted by Peter Paul Rubens in 1634, which hangs above the altar. Rubens' own baby son is said to have been the model for the baby Jesus.

The exhibition, reached through the north door of the choir, giving the history of the building.

Outside, you can walk round the chapel to Scholar's Piece, part of the Backs (see page 33), and look back for that famous view that adorns Christmas cards and prints of the chapel in all its Perpendicular glory.

**Open:** daily – check boards outside the main gate for times
**Entry:** under £5
**Tel:** 01223 331100/331212
**Website:** www.kings.cam.ac.uk

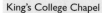

was placed here in 1879 – more than four centuries after the foundation of King's in 1441. The young king founded his college exclusively for scholars from Eton and much of the medieval town was destroyed to make way for it. Henry laid the foundation stone for his chapel in 1446 but the building wasn't completed until almost 70 years later. The fan-vaulted ceiling is breathtaking in its scope, while the stained-glass windows were made and installed during the reign of Henry VIII. They were removed for safekeeping during the Second World War.

King's College Chapel

### Magdalene College
Magdalene Street; map C1

As in 'the other place' (Cambridge and Oxford-speak for each other) the 'g' is silent and you change the vowel sound to pronounce the name of this 450-year-old college 'maudlin'. Magdalene is regarded in some quarters as a little exclusive and sometimes called 'the village'. Students at this college are the only ones to wear white tie and tails at their celebratory May Balls – the others make do with the more usual black tie.

### DON'T MISS
The famous Pepys Library where each of the 3,000 books left by the diarist is arranged from 1 to 3,000 by size. Samuel Pepys, who was at Magdalene from 1651–54, insisted that his collection, which includes his six volumes of diaries, should remain entire – neither added to nor subtracted from.

**Open:** daily 9.00–18.00;
Pepys Library: daily; early Oct–mid-Mar: 14.30–15.30; late April–end Aug: 11.30–12.30, 14.30–15.30
**Tel:** 01223 332100
**Website:** www.magd.cam.ac.uk

Magdalene College

> **SITTING PRETTY**
> Until the late 18th century, all examinations at Cambridge were oral; a student would have to debate or dispute a subject with an 'examiner' who always sat on a three-legged stool, or 'tripos'. Hence the peculiar Cambridge expression 'tripos' for today's written exams.

### Museum of Archaeology and Anthropology
Downing Street; map E5

Outstanding collections from around the world are of interest to scholars and visitors alike. You can trace human development from earliest times to when we started reading and writing. Art and culture from many regions of the world are shown, while photographs spanning more than 100 years are on display too.

**Open:** Tue–Sat 14.00–16.30. Closed one week at Christmas and Easter
**Entry:** free
**Tel:** 01223 333516
**Website:** www.archanth.cam.ac.uk
**Disabled access:** please telephone before your visit
**Other facilities:** shop

Museum of Archaeology and Anthropology

**Open:** Mon–Fri 10.00–17.00, Sat (term time only) 10.00–13.00
**Entry:** free
**Tel:** 01223 335153
**Website:** www.classics.cam.ac.uk/ark
**Disabled access:** full

Pembroke College

### Pembroke College
Trumpington Street; map C6
The gatehouse here is the oldest in Cambridge. They open the gates early and you're free to wander through the beautiful grounds and enjoy the courts. Visit the chapel, which is the first complete piece of work by Christopher Wren. The third oldest college,

### Museum of Classical Archaeology
Sidgwick Avenue; map A6
Why go to Greece and Italy to see classical statues and sculptures when the 'Ark' in Cambridge has plaster-cast reproductions of all the major pieces? More than 600 casts have been gathered together as teaching material, but visitors are welcome to enjoy them too.

Museum of Classical Archaeology

Pembroke was founded in 1337 by the sad Marie St Pol de Valence, the widowed Countess of Pembroke, whose husband was killed in a joust on their wedding day.

**Open:** daily, dawn to dusk; group visits 14.00–17.00
**Entry:** free
**Tel:** 01223 338100
**Website:** www.pem.cam.ac.uk

Peterhouse

### ALARMED BY FIRE

Poet Thomas Gray (best known for his 'Elegy written in a country churchyard') had such a morbid fear of fire that he built a rudimentary fire escape in the shape of a metal bar to take a rope ladder on the window of his rooms in Peterhouse. It is said that he used it once, when a hoax fire alarm was raised by unkind pranksters, but was so upset by the experience that he moved from Peterhouse, where he had been both an undergraduate and a don, to Pembroke College.

## Peterhouse College
### Trumpington Street

This is Cambridge's oldest college, founded nearly 800 years ago in 1284. Not much of the original building remains – the hall, largely restored in the 19th century, is the only 13th-century room left. You can see it and the chapel and enjoy the gardens and old courts. Several Peterhouse students have had an innovative streak – Charles Babbage, Sir Frank Whittle and Sir Christopher Cockerell, inventors respectively of the computer, jet engine and hovercraft, all studied here.

**Open:** daily 9.00–17.00
**Entry:** free
**Tel:** 01223 338200
**Website:** www.pet.cam.ac.uk

Peterhouse

Queens' College

### Queens' College
Queens' Lane; map C6

Those punctilious about grammar should be assured that the apostrophe in Queens' is correctly placed – two queens were involved in the foundation of this medium-sized college, spoilt only, some would say, by the addition of the white concrete Cripps building in 1974. But you'll like Old Court with its medieval brickwork and the half-timbered 16th-century President's Lodge in Cloister Court. Erasmus's Tower is the obvious name for the building where the great scholar lived and worked. The original of the much photographed but rather rickety-looking wooden bridge was designed by William Etheridge and built according to 'mathematical principles' (whose we don't know) and is therefore called the Mathematical Bridge. The two founder queens were Margaret of Anjou, wife of Henry VI, and Elizabeth Woodville, Edward IV's queen and mother of the two princes murdered in the Tower of London.

**Open:** times and charges vary according to time of year – ring for details
**Tel:** 01223 335511
**Website:** www.qus.cam.ac.uk

### Round Church
Bridge Street; map D2

Round Church

You'll have no difficulty finding this one – it's obviously round and stands on the corner where Bridge Street meets Round Church Street. Round churches were built in the 12th century to commemorate the Church of the

Holy Sepulchre in Jerusalem. They were built with circular naves and aisles and a small chancel. It was altered in the 15th century and 'restored' with the addition of a conical roof in the 19th and is the oldest of the four round churches remaining in Britain. It is, in fact, properly called the Church of the Holy Sepulchre but most people just call it the Round Church. It's open daily but is not now in regular use for services.

**Open:** daily, Tue–Sat 10.00–17.00, Sun–Mon 13.00–17.00
**Entry:** free
**Tel:** 01223 331602
**Disabled access:** limited

### St Bene't's Church
Bene't Street; map D5
This little Anglo-Saxon church tucked

St Bene't's Church

away in a tiny garden is notable in that its tower is the oldest building in the county of Cambridgeshire – thought to have been built in 1025 during the reign of King Canute. It is very likely too that the first properly organized and devised peal of bells was rung from here in the mid-17th century. Fabian Stedman, the mathematically minded parish clerk of St Bene't's, was the 'inventor' of change-ringing as we know it today. There are six bells, the earliest dated 1588 and the latest 1825 and they are still rung weekly. The church has strong links with nearby Corpus Christi College.

**Open:** daily 7.30–18.30, Holy Eucharist daily at 8.00
**Entry:** free
**Tel:** 01223 353903
**Website:** www.e-cambridge.co.uk/ stbenets
**Disabled access:** limited

### St Catharine's College
Trumpington Street
St Catharine's is one of the smaller colleges. It is named for Catharine of Alexandria, condemned for her faith to be crucified on a wheel, which shattered as she touched it – look for the Catharine-wheel emblem on the gate. Inside the college you can see the chapel and the courts. John Addenbrooke, who read medicine here in the 1690s, left money in his will to found the world-famous Addenbrooke's Hospital.

**Open:** daily 9.00–16.00 except May–mid-June (during exams)
**Entry:** free
**Tel:** 01223 338300
**Website:** www.caths.cam.ac.uk

## St John's College
**St John's Street; map C2**

Visitors cross the road so that they can take a long look at the magnificent gatehouse of this, the second college founded by Lady Margaret Beaufort, mother to King Henry VII. Two glorious gilded yales – mythical beasts with the heads of goats, bodies of antelopes and elephants' tails – support her coat of arms, while the marguerite daisies symbolize her name. St John stands in a niche above. You can also see yales on the gateway to Lady Margaret's first foundation, Christ's College (see page 36).

There's much to admire in St John's (founded 1511). You'll pass through a fine series of courts to reach the 'Kitchen Bridge' across the Cam. From here you can watch punters with varying degrees of skill negotiate the waters underneath the neo-Gothic 'Bridge of Sighs' and the bends in the river to the south. A stroll along the gravelled paths takes you round the well-tended gardens and towards the Backs (see page 33). St John's was the college that instigated the annual Oxford and Cambridge boat race, when they threw out a challenge to Oxford in 1829.

**DON'T MISS**
The fine linen-fold carving on the panels of the gates.
The chapel, where Hugh Ashton, an early Fellow of St John's, is shown twice on his tomb – once dressed in finery and again as an emaciated corpse.

**Open:** Easter–early Nov: Mon–Fri 10.00–17.00, Sat–Sun 9.30–17.00; normally open during winter (ring to check)
**Entry:** under £5
**Tel:** 01223 338600
**Website:** www.joh.cam.ac.uk

Scott Polar Research Institute

## Scott Polar Research Institute
Lensfield Road

'He sought the secret of the pole, but found the hidden face of God' is the translation of the Latin inscription on the front of the building housing the museum, which exhibits letters, papers, drawings, equipment and all things linked to expeditions to the poles of the Earth. The 'he' is Captain Robert Falcon Scott RN who perished with his companions in 1912. The Institute was founded in his memory in 1920 and has grown to become the most important polar archive in the world. It now includes the Shackleton Memorial Library. The museum attached to the Institute is open year-round.
**Open:** Tue–Sat 14.30–16.00
**Entry:** free
**Tel:** 01223 336555
**Website:** www.spri.cam.ac.uk
**Disabled access:** full
**Other facilities:** shop

## Sedgwick Museum of Earth Sciences
Downing Street; map E5

Named for Adam Sedgwick, Cambridge Woodwardian Professor of Geology from 1818–73 and the man who inspired the young Charles Darwin, this fascinating museum has more than one million fossils in its collection. Here is evidence of the earliest forms of life from more than 3,000 million years ago to the remains of the creatures that roamed the fens a mere 150,000 years ago. Arachnophobes won't like 'Big Meg' – a hairy reconstruction of the world's largest spider, *Megarachne servinei*. Her leg span is 50 cm (20 in) and her body is 10 cm (4 in) across. The good news is that she lived 300 million years ago. The exhibits include geologist John Woodward's entire fossil collection, housed in its original walnut cabinets.
**Open:** Mon–Fri 9.00–13.00, 14.00–17.00; Sat 10.00–13.00
**Entry:** free
**Tel:** 01223 333456
**Website:** www.sedgwickmuseum.org
**Disabled access:** full

---

**B LAZING JACKETS**
Members of the famed Lady Margaret Boat Club, rowing men and women from St John's College, are well known about town for their scarlet jackets. It was the vivid colour of these coats that gave rise to the term 'blazer' well over 100 years ago.

Sidney Sussex College

### Sidney Sussex College
Sidney Street; map E3
Oliver Cromwell studied here for just
12 months (1616–17) but had to leave
to support his family on his father's
death. Visitors can see the chapel, the
courts and the gardens.
**Open:** daily 9.00–17.00
**Entry:** free
**Tel:** 01223 338800
**Website:** www.sid.cam.ac.uk

### Trinity College
Trinity Street; map C3
You can shorten the odds on receiving
a Nobel Prize by gaining a place at
Cambridge's largest college, Trinity, which
has nurtured 31 Nobel prizewinners.
Thomas Nevile's (Master 1593–1615)
magnificent Great Court, which covers
0.8 hectares (2 acres), was the scene
for the race between Harold Abrahams
and Lord Burghley shown in the film

Trinity College sundial

*Chariots of Fire*. That race never actually took place, although Lord Burghley did accomplish the almost impossible feat of running round the entire court in the time it took the clock (which strikes the hours twice over) to sound out noon. That was in 1927 and undergraduates today still try to beat the clock.

Founded by Henry VIII in 1546, Trinity has many famous names on its roll of honour, including mathematician and philosopher Sir Isaac Newton (his statue stands in the ante-chapel), Lord Macaulay, Alfred Lord Tennyson, Thackeray – and Christopher Robin, son of A.A. Milne.

The great Wren Library, designed by Christopher Wren and completed in 1695, holds many notable manuscripts from an 8th-century copy of the Epistles of St Paul to the original *Winnie-the-Pooh*. There is a punting station at Trinity, where you can hire punts to explore the Backs. Oh – and if you think that the statue of Henry VIII above the Great Gate is clutching what appears to be a sturdy chair leg, you'd be right. Students again.

**Open:** Mar–Oct: daily 10.00–16.30; Nov–Feb: times vary (ring to check)
Wren Library: during vacation Mon–Fri: 12.00–14.00; during term 10.30–12.30
**Entry:** under £5; entry via the Garret Hostel Lane gate (map B3) is free for those using the punting station
Wren Library: free (use the Garret Hostel Lane gate; map B3)
**Tel:** 01223 338400
**Website:** www.trin.cam.ac.uk

### University Museum of Zoology
Downing Street; map E5

Just head for the spectacular whale skeleton above the entrance and you're on course for a unique collection of fossils, skeletons large and small, British birds and beautiful shells. Many of the specimens are those collected by Charles Darwin as he gathered evidence that led to his theory of evolution. Recent refurbishment has created spacious and light galleries that show the collections well.

**Open:** 21 Jun–end Sep: Mon–Fri 10.00–16.45, Sat 10.00–13.00; Oct–20 Jun: Mon–Fri 10.00–16.45
**Entry:** free
**Tel:** 01223 336650

**Website:** www.zoo.cam.ac.uk
**Disabled access:** full

### Whipple Museum of the History of Science
Free School Lane; map D5

If you want to see how scientific measurements were made in the Middle Ages, this museum with its collection of instruments and models spanning the centuries is the place to go. Sundials, early slide rules, microscopes, telescopes and calculators of all sorts are housed in several galleries. The main exhibition space is an imposing hall with an Elizabethan hammer-beam ceiling.

**Open:** during term: Mon–Fri 13.30–16.30; during vacations – ring to check
**Entry:** free
**Tel:** 01223 334500
**Website:** www.hps.cam.ac.uk/whipple
**Disabled access:** full, but telephone in advance

Whipple Museum of the History of Science

Jesus Green

# BREATHING SPACE

If you want a breath of fresh air, Cambridge is your city. Huge areas of green space, many of them along the banks of the River Cam, provide places to picnic, play and stroll.

### The Backs; map B2–B6

The most famous green space is the Backs (see page 33) – the land bordering the far ends of the riverside colleges. A favourite picnic place and walk, the Backs is a mix of tussocky grass grazed by cattle, smooth lawns, immaculate gardens and a mass of flowers in the spring. You can reach the Backs by a footpath in Silver Street, past the

**WHAT'S IN A NAME?**
You'll see that the River Granta is now a
tributary of the Cam – but there was a time
when the whole river was called 'Granta'.
No one is sure when the change came
about but the name 'Granta' still crops up
a lot in Cambridge.

Jesus Lock

land bought by the
Council from Jesus
College over 100 years
ago. This large space
contains gardens, a bowl-
ing green, tennis courts
and a children's play area.

### Parker's Piece

This is where the great
cricketer Jack Hobbs prac-
tised his craft and where
he is remembered today
with three cricket pitches
and a pavilion restaurant
that bears his name.
The land is named after
Edward Parker who used
to farm it.

### College gardens

Some college gardens
open to the public will
surprise you with their
beauty. Christ's, Clare
and Emmanuel are partic-
ularly lovely, while King's,
Magdalene, Peterhouse
and St John's are all definitely worth visiting if you
get the chance.

### Round Church

You'll see the Round
Church (Church of the
Holy Sepulchre) on the
corner of Bridge Street.
The garden is tiny but
it provides a seat and
a peaceful space in the
bustle of the city.

Mathematical Bridge on
your right (see page 48)
and past the new buildings
of Queens'. Turn right into
Queens' Green and follow
the riverside walk behind
Queens', King's, Clare,
Trinity and St John's.

### Laundress Green;
map C6

You reach Laundress
Green at the bottom of
Mill Lane. This is a hugely
popular 'island' bordered
by the mill pool. It is
named for the washer
women of Cambridge
who used to rent space
here to hang their laundry
to dry. People come to
picnic, enjoy a drink, or
simply to sit and watch

the efforts of the punters
working their way along
the water.

### Jesus Green;
map E1

Much larger than
Laundress Green is Jesus
Green. There are acres of
space here, which include
an impressive avenue of
plane trees leading to the
delightful Jesus Lock, a
large outdoor swimming
pool, tennis courts, bowl-
ing green and children's
play area as well.

### Christ's Pieces;
map F3

The name might sound a
little strange but the area
is made up from pieces of

# SHOPPING

Cambridge is a shopper's paradise. If you're looking for something special, a present, books or clothes for an occasion, the chances are you'll find it. But watch those impulse buys: there are so many individual shops offering lovely things that you can easily start snapping up unconsidered trifles, making your wallet a whole lot lighter.

Because the centre of the city is virtually a car-free zone, dodging from one street to another is easy. Watch out for bicycles though – they sail up on you silently as you hurry across the road to peer in yet another enchanting window. Some of the individual shops are listed below, but you'll spot more as you explore the streets and lanes. High-Street names are to be found in the new Grafton Centre, in Lion Yard Shopping Centre (map E4) and in Sidney Street (map D2–E4).

MARR
THE BEST LITT
LEATHER SHO
IN ENGLAN

Marrs (page 62)

Heffers bookshop (page 61)

### Shopping hours

High-Street shops tend to open from 9.00 to 17.30. Many of the smaller family-owned shops don't open until 10.00. Wednesday sees some of the larger stores open late while, in the summer and before Christmas, many shops open on Sundays.

### Books and music

As you'd expect in a great university city there's a wide range of bookshops, many of them with their own particular character.

### Green Street; map D3

Here is a branch of the American store Borders, which sells books and music. Across the lane is specialist shop Brian Jordan selling books, music and print music for a huge range of instruments.

### King's Parade; map D4

This is where you'll find Inner Space with books on meditation and things felt but not always seen.

### Magdalene Street; map C1

An excellent second-hand bookshop, called simply The Bookshop, is found at No. 24, opposite Magdalene College. Bang & Olufsen music systems are nearby.

### Rose Crescent; map D3

MDC Classic Music is to be found in this pretty pedestrian walkway.

### St Andrew's Street; map F5

Here is Heffers Plus with cards and gift wrap in addition to the books.

### St Edward's Passage; map D4

Not one but two excellent second-hand bookshops in this narrow twisting lane connecting Peas Hill with King's Parade. The so-called 'Haunted Bookshop' (they're diffident about the ghost who is supposed to walk up and down the stairs) specializes in illustrated editoins and children's books (remember

G.David

*The Chalet School* and *Just William*?). Once you start reading in here, you'll never stop. It looks small and it is. Just a few steps away is G. David, on the other hand, which looks small, but isn't. It offers lots of choice in several rambling rooms.

### Sidney Street; map D2–E4

There's a good branch of Waterstone's here, while bargain-hunters will probably find the book they're seeking at Galloway and Porter. Fopp Music, part of a small independent chain, is here too, selling CDs, DVDs and vinyl. At No. 28 the Oxfam Bookshop has a good selection and a high turnover.

### Sussex Street; map E3

Two music shops in one here – the combination of Miller's Music Centre and the jointly owned Ken Stevens next door means you can buy anything from sheet music for bagpipes to the latest guitar and all the instruments for a complete band.

### Trinity Street; map D3

This is home to Heffers, which was to Cambridge what Blackwell's is to

Oxford, with several outlets in the city. Now it is owned by Blackwell's, having been bought a few years ago, but it still retains its well-respected name. When you've found the book you want, move on down the road to Heffers Sound to buy music. On the corner of Trinity Street and St Mary's Street stands the Cambridge University Press bookshop, which has been selling books for more than 400 years.

Ally Lulu (page 62)

### Fashion

Cambridge does lots of things well – but it excels itself when it comes to clothes and accessories for both men and women.

### Bene't Street; map D5

A small but appealing street, with a good arts

and craft shop, a pub full of history and several fashion shops, including Christiane Roberts, where you should find something unusual and individual for special occasions. Frank Clothes and Reeves cater for a younger, trendier market. Dream on at La Reve, with glamorous lingerie from La Perla and Rigby and Peller.

### Green Street; map D3

You could spend all day here – there's Javelin with

a window full of lovely dresses and bags, while Pachamama has brightly coloured cotton skirts, dresses from Bali and

Hero

Baska Design

a small boutique with designer names, and Gun Hill, where you'll find that elusive 'smart-casual' outfit.

### Magdalene Street; map C1

This is home to Baska Design, full of unusual and beautiful hats, many made by the owner. Just down the road is Bowns, for classic clothes and special-occasion dresses.

### Rose Crescent; map D3

This pretty curving street is home to Marrs (who call themselves 'the best little leather shop in England') with lovely coloured leather bags, belts, gloves and luggage too. Sandra Kent is a

chunky hand-knitted sweaters, which are just the thing for a cold fenland winter. If it's the great outdoors you're taking on, visit Patagonia for the latest walking gear and outdoor clothing. Catfish (the girlie version of Dogfish in Trinity Street) is bound to tempt you inside while there is no way you won't be drawn into Ally Lulu with bags, shoes, purses and scarves to die for. Across the way is Hero, under the same ownership and full of designer clothes by Ghost, Amanda Wakeley, Nicole Farhi, philosophy, Fornarina and Vivienne Westwood. Sundaes and Ecco have lots of deliciously soft leather shoes.

### King's Parade; map D4

Newly spruced-up, one of Cambridge's smartest streets is home to Troon,

The Tailor's Cat (page 64)

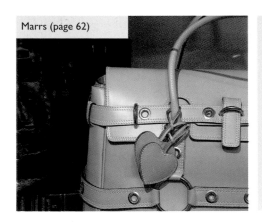
Marrs (page 62)

**TREAT YOURSELF**
Absolutely THE place to buy your bow tie is Anthony in Trinity Street. No matter that you never wear one – you will, once you see the stunning range of choice.

boutique that stocks Escada, St John and Laurel, while classy Hampstead Bazaar is nearby.

**St John's Street; map D2**
Amanda Green is the shoe shop to look for here – it has plenty of different styles displayed on two floors.

**The Shopping Forum, Jesus Lane; map E2**
Milk (for men and women) sells trendy streetwear while Countryside specializes in – you've guessed it – outdoor gear.

**Sussex Street; map E3**
The Tailor's Cat is full of very feminine clothes – just the sort of things for

parties, May Balls and romantic dates.

**Trinity Street; map D3**
You're spoilt for choice with Hobbs, Rohan, Phase Eight, Viyella, Laura Ashley, Jaeger, Diesel and Reiss, the latter in a beautiful building. Dogfish is just

the place for clothes-conscious men to shop, while Anthony is the honeypot where some television presenters and nearly all of Cambridge buy their ties and (hand-tied) bow ties – and jackets, trousers and shirts to go with them.

Amanda Green

Anthony

The Cambridge Cheese Company

**Food and drink**
**All Saints Passage; map D2**
Two of Cambridge's most tempting shops stand next door to each other in this tiny walkway. The Cambridge Cheese Company sells not only a huge range of fresh English cheeses but also locally produced bacon ('If I was a pig, I'd be proud,' reads the sign) and treats such as little jars of caviar. Then you must visit the Bellina Chocolate House, sniff the air and set about buying. They do chocolates for diabetics too, which taste as good as the others.

**King's Parade; map D4**
Fudge Kitchen is not to be missed as they make the delicious sweet stuff on the premises and you can watch them doing it.

**The Shopping Forum, Jesus Lane; map E2**
Fujifood is Cambridge's only Japanese grocery store – buy all the ingredients for your sushi here.

Bellina Chocolate House

Fudge Kitchen

## Galleries and gift shops

### Bene't Street; map D5

Arcadia is a small gallery selling the best of British. All their craft pieces (hand-painted cufflinks, ceramics, clocks and mirrors) are sourced from artists living and working in the British Isles.

### Castle Street: map C1

The Cambridge and County Folk Museum (see page 35) has a gift shop specializing in reproduction Victorian toys such as spinning tops, slates and toy theatres.

### Green Street; map D3

Chaps of Cambridge has lots of boys' toys.

Cambridge Contemporary Art

Primavera

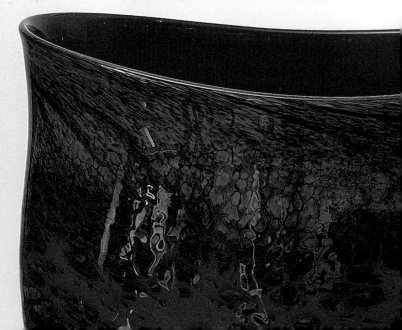

### King's Parade; map D4

Primavera claims to be Britain's oldest contemporary art and craft gallery with a well-earned reputation for pieces from artists of repute. At any one time you'll find jewellery, ceramics, glassware, furniture, textiles and a lot more. Next door is The Lawson Gallery, selling paintings and prints. Nomads sells objects bought in from around the world.

### Magdalene Street; map C1

Art-d.co.uk sells — well, yes, original and reproduction art deco ceramics. You'll find Susie Cooper here and some Clarice Cliff and plenty more

Art-d.co.uk

besides from the Staffordshire Potteries, including work by modern artists and designers too.

### Rose Crescent; map D3

You might find a present at The Crystal Shop or at Wow, which has lots of trendy Italian houseware. If you're into games of all sorts, visit Lingards which has the lot from Cadoo to mah-jong, Cranium to Monopoly. Beautiful presents from the best olive oil to scented bath oils, soaps and cosmetics are to be found at L'Occitane en Provence.

### The Shopping Forum, Jesus Street; map E2

Here you'll find two arty shops. Art Gecko specializes in silver jewellery, while Inside Out has lots of contemporary furniture for homes and gardens.

### Trinity Street; map D3

Cambridge Contemporary Art shows modern works by living artists. Paintings, glass, ceramics are all new and exciting. Across the road, Breeze sells contemporary glass and china and objects that will look good in your house or garden.

### Jewellery

**Rose Crescent; map D3**
Cellini's is the place to visit
if you want to buy pearls.

**St John's Street; map D2**
Toko has a window full of
lovely pieces of contem-
porary silver jewellery.

**The Shopping Forum,
Jesus Street; map E2**
Art Gecko also specializes
in silver jewellery.

**Trinity Street; map D3**
Buckies specializes in silver;
they do valuations too.

### Markets

**The Market, Market Hill;
map D4**
Cambridge has a splendid
open-air market from
Monday to Saturday
(9.30–16.30), where
you can buy just about
anything from ball gowns
to fresh fish, fruit, vegeta-
bles and flowers. The
Bikeman will mend your
trusty two-wheeler while
you refresh yourself with
freshly squeezed juice or
sip a pick-me-up espresso
from the aptly named
Caffé Mobile. On Sundays
the Farmers' Market and
the Arts, Crafts and
Antiques Market take over
from 10.30–16.30.

Arcadia (page 66)

L'Occitane en Provence (page 67)

# EATING AND DRINKING

Even if you don't punt yourself, watching other people poling their way up and down the river gives you an appetite. As you would expect, there are plenty of cafés, pubs and good restaurants to keep hunger at bay.

Cambridge is a city full of open space and you'll notice that many people take advantage of the shops selling baguettes, filled rolls and sandwiches to eat outside. The ice cream sold by the street vendors is the real thing and it's also worth buying a coffee from the enterprising Caffé Mobile – coffee-on-the-move – who dispense good coffee; one van operates from the market, while the other can often be found opposite the main entrance to St John's College. You can also buy fresh fruit juices and smoothies from a stall in the market.

Refreshments in the market

## CAFES

As you explore the city you'll see the usual coffee-shop chains – Starbucks, Café Nero and so on. There's a café cluster at Quayside (map C1) where you can also hire a punt.

The Little Tea Room

### All Saint's Passage; map D2

The Little Tea Room is a bit of a misnomer as it can actually serve quite a lot of people in a series of small rooms. It also does a good breakfast.

### King Street; map F3

Clowns is named after the Italian owner's favourite Italian opera, *Il Pagliaccio*, and it's a lovely friendly, busy place with excellent coffee, pasta and cakes. It opens early (good breakfasts) and closes late.

### Market Street and St Mary's Passage; map D4

Here on a corner of the marketplace are chairs set outside in all but the nastiest of weathers for those taking coffee and a pastry at Don Pasquale. There's space indoors too and upstairs you can eat pizza. Auntie's, with its uniformed waitresses, lacy tablecloths and china-filled cabinets, is much loved by many – especially for the famous cream teas (scones, cream, jam and tiny sandwiches). You can sit outside here too in good weather and keep an eye on King's College.

### Pembroke Street; map D6

There's a wonderful atmosphere in the tiny, colourful Trockel Ulmann und Freunde tucked away off the main drag. It's worth visiting this off-beat café for the excellent coffee and the delicious home-made cakes (crumbly confections filled with apricot, plum and apple) and equally delicious soup that simmers on the stove behind the counter. The high stools are a bit challenging but the food and the cheerful feel of the place make the clamber well worthwhile.

### St Edward's Passage; map D4

You have a choice of cafés in this tiny passageway, which also has two excellent bookshops and a tiny church that you can visit.

Trockel Ulmann und Freunde

The Michael House Café

O'Brien's Sandwich Bar does coffee too, while the deep blue (what else?) Indigo Coffee House also offers good things to eat. It is bigger than it looks.

## Trinity Street; map D3

Where else would you find an ancient wall painting in the ladies loo and an old gravestone in the gents? The Michael House Café inside the converted St Michael's Church is a meeting place, an exhibition space, and a much-sought-after coffee and lunch venue. It's light, airy, interesting – and the food's good. If it's a full English breakfast you're after, go to Café Trinity, just down the road.

## Trumpington Street

Who hasn't heard of Fitzbillies and its famous Chelsea buns? These sugar-soaked confections are as unlike the pale imitations sold everywhere else as the Koh-i-noor diamond is your average engagement ring. Don't plan on doing too much for an hour or so after eating one. That said, Fitzbillies does delicious lunch and tea, and you can read the newspapers here.

**BAKE ME A CAKE**
There are times when nothing but cake will do. These are the times to indulge yourself at the colourful Trockel Ulmann und Freunde café in Pembroke Street where the home-made cakes are moist, crumbly and delicious. Or visit Fitzbillies in Trumpington Street for a Chelsea bun.

Fitzbillies

## SANDWICH BARS, DELICATESSENS

**All Saints Passage; map D2**
The Cambridge Cheese Company does all sorts of other deli-type goodies as well as a wide range of cheese – haggis and caviar anyone? You can put together the ingredients for a lovely picnic here.

**Rose Crescent; map D3**
Here is the original Peppercorns with a counter stuffed full of different breads and imaginative fillings. There is another, newer, branch in King's Parade.

**Trumpington Street; map D6**
Sam Smiley's your man here for sandwiches and baguettes and other takeaway food.

Hobbs Pavilion

## RESTAURANTS
**Modern English, Mediterranean, French**

**Browns**
**Trumpington Road**
Browns is Browns whether you're in Oxford, Bristol or Cambridge and its brasserie-style cooking and laid-back service are always popular. This Browns has the same

colonial feel as the others, with lush greenery and a grand piano, but those who've lived in Cambridge for a long time know the building was once part of the old Addenbrookes Hospital. You'll enjoy it very much whether you go for the full three-course treatment or just opt for a hot ciabatta sandwich, a plate of pasta

or afternoon tea outside.
Tel: 01223 461655

**Café Adriatic**
**12 Norfolk Street**
Once inside the unprepossessing building you'll like the clean light feel of this small restaurant serving good fish and meat grills, pastas and risottos. It's a local favourite.
Tel: 01223 355227

## Hobbs Pavilion
## Parker's Piece

Tribute is paid in this beautifully converted cricket pavilion to the great Jack Hobbs, cricketer, who played here and used the building regularly. There's a portrait of him and a 'board of honour' showing his cricketing achievements. Here you can enjoy Mediterranean-style food, looking out onto one of Cambridge's pleasant green spaces.
Tel: 01223 367480

## Loch Fyne
## The Little Rose
## Trumpington Street

Excellent fish (with a few options for carnivores) in this converted pub opposite the Fitzwilliam Museum. Good fish-friendly wines too.
Tel: 01223 362433

## Midsummer House
## Midsummer Common

In a lovely secluded setting, the pretty conservatory makes a splendid dining room. For lunch you choose from a set menu which may include ravioli of salmon and langoustine, or ballotine of chicken, while dinner (à la carte) is sometimes pretty

adventurous — deep fried snails, or ravioli of quail and Serrano ham, or pressed terrine of confit of rabbit with fois gras and prune d'agen. For the really adventurous the chef offers an innovative 'tasting menu' to be tried by the whole table.
Tel: 01223 369299

## Restaurant 22
## 22 Chesterton Road

It's easy to miss the front door of this attractive Victorian town house, so get good directions when you book. It's small (seats 26 in the main restaurant) and holds a Michelin Bib Gourmande. You'll be offered starters such as melon soup with prawn, coriander and chilli salsa, French onion tart with rocket and parmesan, or assiette of smoked fish with horseradish cream. Main courses might include roast monkfish

on mascarpone and herb risotto with red wine glaze, or lamb's liver on leek and bacon dauphinoise with roast beetroot.
Tel: 01223 351880

## The Three Horseshoes
## High Street, Madingley

This pretty building, tucked into a corner of the village street a couple of miles to the west of the city, looks like a pub until you step inside. There is a bar, sure, but it's full of nicely laid-out tables which are generally full of eager diners, because the food is delicious and the wine list very good. There's a restaurant, too, in a conservatory but the food is the same wherever you sit. You'll find good pasta with interesting fresh vegetable sauces, delicious locally sourced meat and interesting combinations such as a tempura made of sweet potato and

### TIME FOR TEA

Wherever you may travel never be surprised, even in Timbuktu, to be offered a Fitzbillies' Chelsea bun. The Cambridge bakery receives regular orders for their famous sugar-soaked confections from customers the world over, homesick for their teatime treat. You can order through their website (www.fitzbillies.com).

The Three Horseshoes (page 75)

avocado. Try tamarillo crumble and white chocolate ice cream.
Tel: 01954 210221

## Italian
### Trattoria Pasta Fresca
### 66 Mill Road
Cheerful service and good pasta, pizza and vegetable dishes prompted nomination for a 'pasta restaurant of the year' award. If you've got room, the puddings are delicious too.
Tel: 01223 352836

## Thai
Dojo Noodle Bar
Mill Lane; map C6

This cheerful restaurant, serving 'Pacific Rim' dishes from tempura prawns to Goi Cuon, delights students and other residents and visitors alike with the well-flavoured and inventive menu. If you don't like noodles with your Thai, Japanese or Vietnam food, don't worry – they are happy to bring you rice to eat with it instead.
Tel: 01223 363471

## Vegetarian
The Rainbow Café-Bistro
King's Parade; map D4
Cheerful rainbow signs lead you down a small passageway to bright orange steps and this vegetarian and vegan restaurant, which has an inventive menu ranging from fragrantly spiced fava bean tagine, Tuscan tagliatelle, Latvian potato bake to Peshwari curry. The menu has plenty too for people with gluten and dairy intolerances.
Tel: 01223 321551

## PUBS
Here is a selection of some Cambridge favourites – you'll find others since there are plenty to choose from.

## The Anchor, Silver Street; map C6

This riverside pub is a great favourite with its sunny terrace and view of punts drifting past. It's a rabbit warren inside and even though it's very popular you should be able to find somewhere to sit and enjoy the traditional pub food and real ale.

## Cambridge Blue, Gwydir Street

Although tucked away, this pub is a lovely uncluttered, no-smoking, friendly establishment, serving home-made food a cut above usual pub fare. Small breweries supply the real ale (they'll let you taste before you buy) and there's a good-sized garden for children.

### HOBSON'S CHOICE

Carrier Thomas Hobson had his stables in King's Parade and hired out his horses in strict rotation – you had the next horse in line or none at all – hence the expression 'Hobson's choice'.

## The Bun Shop, King Street; map F3

The name doesn't sound much like a pub and it almost isn't. Upstairs there's a lively tapas bar while downstairs contains a pub bar and a wine bar. It may sound like a bad case of split personality but it seems to work. Many people have a pre-tapas drink downstairs before moving up to eat.

### Champion of the Thames, King Street; map F3

A strange name for a Cambridge pub (perhaps it's wishful thinking), but customers like the 'local' feel, the lunchtime sandwiches and the pub's welcoming atmosphere.

### The Eagle, Bene't Street; map D5

This pub is famous for its low-ceilinged bar, where wartime airmen scrawled signatures and messages on the ceiling with cigarette-lighter flames before they flew off to do battle. Now you can enjoy good pub food and drink here in one of the five old rooms or in the pleasant courtyard. Ask why the upstairs window is never closed (pub ghost story).

### Free Press, Prospect Row

Another quiet tucked-away pub (no smoking) with a good simple menu, real ale, lots of wood and home-cooked food.

### The Mill, Mill Lane; map C6

Particularly popular in the summer when you can take your pint (in a plastic glass) onto the riverbank. They do baguettes and jacket potatoes, all reasonably priced.

### The Pickerel Inn, Magdalene Street; map C1

This pub claims to be the oldest in the city. It's certainly old and legend says that its been an opium den, a brothel and a gin palace in its time.

More respectable now, it's a favourite with students and visitors who enjoy the reasonably priced food and good beer.

The Eagle ceiling

The Eagle

# AN EVENING OUT

Concerts, theatre, restaurants and even a punt down the Cam – Cambridge nightlife may be restrained but there's always something going on. There are clubs, too, for the young and young-at-heart; if you want a pleasant evening at a pub or a restaurant there's plenty of choice (see pages 74–78).

### Romance on the river

Real romantics will want to try an evening punt. You can go it alone (not so many people watching in the twilight) or hire a chauffeured punt. If you want to build in a pub meal or a picnic and don't want to be back before 22.00, you can hire your punt overnight – they'll issue you with an ingenious locking device. The punting companies will also make up picnics, from cream teas to Pimms. See page 83 for details.

### A night at the theatre

The Arts Theatre in St Edward's Passage (map D4) hosts professional drama, dance opera and music companies. You can eat here before or after the show. Call them on 01223 503333. That's also the number for the University-based adc theatre in Park Street where the University Dramatic Club presents its productions alongside those of other amateur and professional companies. The stately looking Corn Exchange in Wheeler Street has been transformed into a major venue for concerts and theatre, ballet and opera. Their box office number is 01223 357851.

### Take in a movie

Blockbusters and films on general release can be seen at the Warner Village multiplex cinema at the Grafton Centre. Ring 08702 406020 for programme information. A wide range of 'art' films, new releases, foreign-language films, classics, late-night shows and children's matinees are shown at the Cambridge Arts Picturehouse in St Andrew's Street. Ring 01223 504444 for information and bookings.

### Go to church

Evensong at King's College Chapel is an unforgettable

experience. Look at the boards outside for times. Other colleges, including St John's, also welcome visitors to Evensong.

## Musical interlude

Every college has its choir and music is part of Cambridge life. Whenever you visit the city you should be able to find a concert to enjoy. The Tourist Information Centre (TIC) in Wheeler Street (see page 94) will have details. The University Concert Hall (tel 01223 503333) in West Road and the Corn Exchange (tel 01223 357851) in Wheeler Street are two of the main concert venues.

## A touch of drama

A walking tour with a difference happens every Tuesday and Friday evening during August when you'll encounter famous characters from Cambridge's past. You might bump into Isaac Newton or Henry VIII (hang onto your heads). Telephone the TIC guided tours department on 01223 457574 for details. Tours leave the TIC in Wheeler Street (map D4) at 18.30.

The Anchor

# TOURS AND TRIPS

Cambridge is a small city, virtually car-free and easy to negotiate on foot. There are excellent daily walking tours for individuals, families and groups. Open-top buses give you a good view and, to see the parts you can't reach by land, you can take a chauffeured punt and glide lazily down the river.

Walking tour

## On foot

Join a two-hour walking tour from the Tourist Information Centre (TIC) in Wheeler Street (map D4). A Blue Badge guide will ensure you see King's College and Chapel when they are open and the fee (between £5 and £10) reflects the entrance charge. You can just turn up (although the tours are limited to 20) or book 24 hours ahead. Visit the TIC or telephone 01223 457574 for times and other details.

## Group tours

Cambridge Blue Badge guides have devised a variety of tours for groups, including themed walking tours, treasure hunts, coach tours and evening walking tours.

Visit the TIC in Wheeler Street or telephone 01223 457574 for information. Large parties wanting to visit the colleges should be accompanied by a Blue Badge guide. The Botanic Garden (see page 34) will also organize guided tours for groups, but these must be booked in advance (tel 01223 336265).

## Take a bus
Open-top sightseeing buses tour the city, giving a commentary on the way. They take a circular route every 15–30 minutes, depending on the season, and can be boarded at many points. Buy your ticket on board or at the TIC in Wheeler Street and hop on or off as you like.

## Twice as nice
You can book a combined walking and punting tour – call 01223 457574 for information about times and prices.

## Dramatic encounters
You might meet Isaac Newton or Henry VIII on

the Tuesday and Friday evening drama tours that leave the TIC in Wheeler Street at 18.30.

## On the water
The traditional way to see the Backs – the land behind the riverside colleges – is by punt. You can go it alone or hire someone else to do the hard work. Punts (and rowing boats and canoes) can be hired from Mill Lane (map C6). You can also punt up river to Grantchester from here. The Trinity College punting station is at Garrett Hostel Lane (map B3), while the Quayside punting station (map C1) hires

out boats for the Backs only. There's another, quieter, punting station at Jesus Lock downriver from Quayside. You can also book food and drink (jugs of Pimms go down well) by contacting Scudamores on 01223 359750 or by Internet at www. scudamores.co.uk.

## Horse mad
Telephone 01638 666789 to book a tour of the National Stud at nearby Newmarket. The 75-minute tour takes in the stallion unit, nursery yards and visits the mares and foals in their paddocks. More information on www.nationalstud.co.uk.

RIVER CHAUFFEUR TOURS

# WHAT'S ON

Many university customs have become annual events enjoyed by everyone in the city. Other festivals take place regularly throughout the year. There are also air shows at Duxford (see page 90) and horse racing at Newmarket.

For more information, please contact the Tourist Information Centre in Wheeler Street (map D4). Tel: 0906 5862526 Website: www. tourismcambridge.com

## January
University Lent term starts.
**Pantomime**
Ring the Arts Theatre box office for information; Tel: 01223 503333

## February
Anglesey Abbey

**snowdrop weekend**
At Anglesey Abbey, Lode, 6 miles north-east of Cambridge; Tel: 01223 811200
**Rag Week**
Events throughout the city organized for charity by different colleges.

## March
Lent Bumps
University boat races.
**Lent Term ends.**
**National Science Week**
Ten days of talks, workshops and demonstrations; Tel: 01223 766766

Website: www. admin.cam.ac.uk/univ/ science/
**Wimpole Hall lambing weekends**
At Wimpole Hall, Arrington, 8 miles south-west of Cambridge; Tel: 01223 207257

## April
University Easter term starts.

## May
**Cambridge Beer Festival**
Held in various pubs; Website: www. camra.org.uk/cambridge

## June
**Cambridge Strawberry Fair**
Free one-day festival; Website: www. strawberry-fair.org.uk

### BUMPS IN MAY

May Bumps isn't some ghastly disease peculiar to Cambridge, but four days of boat racing. Lines of 18 boats, separated by one and a half lengths of water, race away at a signal. The aim is to bump the boat in front and move up one place for the next race. If your boat ends at the top of the first division on the fourth day you are 'head of the river'. If you manage four 'bumps' you achieve 'blades'. Oh – and don't expect May Bumps to take place until June.

**College May Balls**
Held (in June) at various colleges to celebrate the end of exams.
**May Bumps**
University boat races (held in June).
**Easter Term ends.**

**July**
**Open Studios**
Around 250 local artists and craftsmen open their studios to the public on weekends throughout July;
Website: www. camopenstudios.co.uk
**Cambridge Folk Festival;**
Tel: 01223 457245
Website: www.cam-folk-fest.co.uk
**City Bumps**
Boat races.
**Pop in the Park**
Pop music and fireworks at Parker's Piece;
Website: www. cambridge.gov.uk/ summer_in_the_city

**July/August**
**Shakespeare Festival**
Six plays held in different college gardens;
Tel: 01223 357851
Website: www.cambridge shakespeare.com

**September**
**Wimpole Hall Heavy Horse Show**
Wimpole Hall, Arrington;
Tel: 01223 207257

**October**
University Michaelmas Term starts.

**November**
Fireworks and funfair
Held on Midsummer Common.

**December**
Michaelmas Term ends.
**Pantomime starts**
Ring the Arts Theatre box office for information;
Tel: 01223 503333
**Festival of Nine Lessons and Carols**
King's College Chapel;
Open to the public, but queues start early;
Website: www. kings.cam.ac.uk /chapel/ ninelessons

May Ball

## THE BEST NIGHT OF THEIR LIVES

Dancing all night in wonderful surroundings, beautiful ball gowns, splendid food, champagne flowing freely – most students' last memories of Cambridge are often the fondest. The May Balls don't actually happen in May but in June, after those dreaded finals are out of the way and celebration is in the air.

# CAMBRIDGE FOR KIDS

On the surface there's not a lot specifically for children in Cambridge, but a look around reveals plenty they are bound to enjoy.

The Folk Museum

### How things used to be

A visit to the Folk Museum (see page 35) will have youngsters' jaws dropping as they see how they would have occupied themselves in the not-so distant past. And, if they like what they see, they can buy replicas of those Victorian spinning tops and toy theatres to try out at home.

### Amazing

Everyone loves a puzzle and the beautiful grass maze at the Botanic Garden (see page 34) will keep kids occupied for quite a time. It is based on the maze that the dreaded Minotaur inhabited in classical Crete. There's nothing as fearsome as that in this one, though, and the 'walls' are made of New Zealand bunch grass. Why not combine the visit with a picnic in the garden for a pleasant day out?

## Making a splash

There's nothing on a hot sunny day like a dip in the open and you and your children can enjoy that in the Jesus Green swimming pool, which is open from June until September. At other times there is the indoor Abbey Swimming Pool at Whitehill Road (off Newmarket Road) or Parkside Pools – complete with flumes – at the junction of Mill Road and Gonville Place.

## Explore the art

The Fitzwilliam Museum (see page 38) has plenty of activities for children from the Hand in Hand family trail, exploring the

Kettle's Yard

collection of handmade objects (free from the main desk), to Professor Quizzing trails, looking at different aspects of the galleries. Younger children will enjoy Heads, Shoulders, Knees and Toes where they can play with laminated cards to piece together figures – or create their own. There are also story-telling sessions and other events suitable for all ages. Ring

the education office at the Museum for more information (01223 332993).

Kettle's Yard (see page 41) also has an active education service with workshops and drawing sessions; tel 01223 352124 for details.

## Top brass

The tales and legends behind some of the brasses that you can rub under the instruction of Kristin Randall make a visit to the Cambridge Brass Rubbing Centre (see page 35) unforgettable. 'Centre' is probably a misnomer as there is no fixed home for the collection, but if you telephone 01223 871621 you can arrange a session that includes a lot of interesting facts too.

Fitzwilliam Museum

## ONLY A ROSE

But what a beauty …
*Rosa x cantabrigiensis* (the
Cambridge Rose) was raised
in 1931 at the Botanic
Gardens and you'll find it
blooming in many college
gardens in the city in April
and May.

# OUT OF TOWN

The fenland countryside around Cambridge may be flat – but it's not dull. Here are a few suggestions to help you explore the area.

American Cemetery

## American Cemetery, Madingley
**2 miles west of Cambridge, on the A1303**

You cannot help but be moved by the peaceful dignity of the rows and rows of nearly 4,000 white crosses. You can walk alongside the pale Portland-stone Wall of the Missing, inscribed with more than 5,000 names of those never found, which ends at the Memorial Chapel. A lone American flag flutters poignantly on a grassy mound in this, the only American Second World War burial ground in Britain. It is open to the public all the year round. Tel: 01954 210350

## DISTANCE MAKES THE HEART GROW FONDER?

It was in 1869 that Emily Davies founded the first women's college in Cambridge. At first it was situated in Hitchin – an inconvenient distance for lecturers to travel. The college soon moved – not to the city, but to its present site at Girton, just over two miles north of the centre. The idea was that it should be near enough for lecturers to reach but far enough away to discourage male students from doing the same. Girton College now admits male and female students.

Ely Cathedral

Tel: 01353 667735
Website: www.
cathedral.ely.anglican.org

## Linton Zoological Gardens, Linton

**10 miles south-east of Cambridge on the A1307**
Mexican red-kneed tarantulas, leopards and tigers all have their place here among 6.5 hectares (16 acres) of gardens.
Tel: 01223 891308
Website:
www.lintonzoo.co.uk

## Audley End House, Audley End, Saffron Walden

**15 miles south-east of Cambridge on the B1383**
You might think this grand house looks a bit palatial – and you'd be right. Audley End is now only around a third of its original size but, when Thomas Howard built a palatial mansion for himself, the reason given was that he had to entertain King James I. Now you can see rooms and furniture designed by Robert Adam, and parkland that was landscaped by 'Capability' Brown.
Tel: 01799 522399 (information line)
Website: www.
english-heritage.org.uk

## Ely Cathedral, Ely

**15 miles north of Cambridge on the A10**
Many people rank this wonderful building, rising majestically out of the flat fens, as their favourite cathedral in Britain. It is not hard to see why. Built on the site of a 7th-century nunnery, the Norman building, topped with its magnificent octagonal lantern, is something to marvel at. There is a museum of stained glass and guided tours can be arranged in summer. There is also a shop, refectory for light refreshment, tea rooms and restaurant.

## Imperial War Museum, Duxford

**10 miles south-east of Cambridge; M11 south-bound, exit 10**
Here, on the site of a historic Battle of Britain airfield, is the largest collection of aircraft – both military and civil – in the country, and the American Air Museum with the best display of historic American aircraft outside the United States. Throughout the year there are special exhibitions, events and displays, while air shows are usually held in May, July (Flying Legends Airshow), September and October.
Tel: 01223 835000
Website: www.iwm.org.uk

## National Stud, Newmarket

**13 miles north-east on the A1303**
A life-size sculpture of the great racehorse Mill Reef takes pride of place at one of the principal studs in the country. You'll meet the stallions before being taken to see the mares and foals – some of them virtually newborn.
Tel: 01638 663464
Website: www.
nationalstud.co.uk

Sheep's Green

# WHERE TO STAY

You can treat yourself to a stay in a grand hotel, a city guest house or book into one of the many good farmhouse bed and breakfasts near the city. The Tourist Information Centre (see page 94) has a complete list of hotels, guest houses, bed and breakfasts, pubs, self-catering cottages and caravan and camp sites. The list below will give you some idea of the range on offer. Check facilities and prices before booking.

### Prices

The £ symbols are an approximate guide for comparing the prices charged for bed and breakfast, which range from less that £50 to over £150 per twin or double room per night.

Cambridge Garden House Moat House

### De-Vere University Arms Hotel
**Regent Street, Cambridge**
Right in the centre of Cambridge, overlooking historic Parker's Piece where batsman Jack Hobbs learned his craft, the University Arms is a luxury hotel with 147

bedrooms in a lovely old building. There's a good restaurant too. Car parking charge.
Tel: 01223 351241
Website: www. devereonline.co.uk
££££

### Cambridge Garden House Moat House
**Granta Place, Cambridge**
The name's a bit of a mouthful but that's to distinguish it from the other Moat House just outside the city. It's a

Wallis Farm

modern building with 117 bedrooms, just 10 minutes from Magdalene Street and backing on to the River Cam, where guests can watch the punts go past and the picnickers on the other bank. Car parking charge.
Tel: 01223 259988
Website: www.moathouse hotels.com
££££

### Meadowcroft Hotel
Trumpington Road, Cambridge
This small country house is 20 minutes' walk from Magdalene Street, Meadowcroft has just 12 bedrooms. This Victorian building is furnished appropriately and set in its own gardens. The hotel is family-run and you will find the service friendly and cheerful.
Tel: 01223 346120

Website: www.meadowcrofthotel.co.uk
£££

### Wallis Farm
Hardwick
Seven ground-floor en-suite twin and double rooms in a converted barn next to the Victorian farmhouse, where breakfast is served at a long table in a sunny dining room. You can self-cater here, too. Six miles from Cambridge and convenient for the Madingley Park and Ride.
Tel: 01954 210347
Website: www.SmoothHound.co.uk/hotels/wallisfarmhouse
££

### Panos Hotel
Hills Road, Cambridge
Only six bedrooms here but lots of personal attention from a friendly and

attentive staff. The award-winning restaurant, which is open to non-residents, serves an unusual but well-praised mix of French and Greek cuisine. Commended for its comfortable bedrooms.
Tel: 01223 212958
Website: www.panoshotel.co.uk
££

### Worth House
Chesterton Road, Cambridge
Only a few minutes' walk from Magdalene Street and the city centre, this roomy, non-smoking, Victorian house offers just two comfortable rooms, one of which can be used as a triple.
Tel: 01223 316074
Website: www.worth-house.co.uk
££

### Upton House
Grange Road
Just one double room with private facilities in this attractive arts and crafts house a little to the west of the city centre. There is parking here too.
Tel: 01223 323201
Email: tom.challis@talk21.com
£

# USEFUL INFORMATION

## TOURIST INFORMATION

Tourist Information Centre (TIC), The Old Library, Wheeler Street, Cambridge CB2 3QB; map D4

Services include accommodation booking, travel, attraction and event information, maps and guides. Open: Easter–Sep: Mon–Fri 10.00–17.30, Sat 10.00–17.00, Sun and bank holidays 11.00–16.00; Oct–Easter: Mon–Fri 10.00–17.30, Sat 10.00–17.00 Tel: 0906 5862526; For accommodation, tel: 01223 457581 Website: www.tourismcambridge.com

## What's On

Check with the TIC for the latest information or buy the *Cambridgeshire Evening News* which lists what's on.

## Guided walking tours

Official guided walking tours lasting two hours leave the TIC daily at,

13.30 throughout the year. Other tours leave at different times, depending on the season. Ring 01223 457574 for information.

## TRAVEL

### By air

Stanstead Airport is a 40-minute drive from Cambridge. Airport information desk: 08700 000303

### By rail

Fast and frequent trains from both London Kings Cross and London Liverpool Street. Connections from the North via Peterborough. Cambridge railway station (Station Road) is near the Botanic Garden, about a mile to the south of the city centre. National rail enquiries: 08457 484950

### By coach and bus

The bus and coach station is at Drummer Street (map F4) in the city centre. There are hourly

National Express Services from London Victoria Coach Station; Tel: 08705 808080 Jetlink run regular bus services from Heathrow, Gatwick, Luton and Stanstead airports; Tel: 08705 747777 for information; 08705 757747 for bookings Local buses are operated by Stagecoach Cambus; Tel: 08706 082608

### Shopmobility

Lion Yard Car Park, 5th floor (map E5), and Grafton Centre East Car Park, 4th floor. Free use of powered scooters and powered and manual wheelchairs. Help is available on arrival, but please phone first. Tel: 01223 457452 (Lion Yard); 01223 461858 (Grafton Centre)

### Taxis

There are taxi ranks at the bus and coach station at Drummer Street (map F4), at the railway station in Station Road, in Emmanuel Street (map F4) and in St Andrews Street (map F5).

**Bike hire**

City Cycle Hire, Newnham Road; Tel: 01223 365629
The Cycle King, Mill Road; Tel: 01223 214999
H. Drake, Hills Road; Tel: 01223 363468
Mike's Bikes, Mill Road; Tel: 01223 312591

## PARK AND RIDE
### map: page 100

Car parking in Cambridge is limited and expensive and much of the city centre is closed to traffic during the day. There is an excellent park and ride system with free parking in five car parks spaced evenly around the city.

The buses leave every 10 minutes from 7.00–20.00. You pay around £1.50 for your return fare. All are clearly signposted from all major approaches to Cambridge. Park and rides are at:
Cowley Road; A1309
Newmarket; A1303
Babraham Road; A1307
Trumpington Road; junction 11 of the M11
Madingley Road; junction 13 of the M11

## BANKS

Abbey National, St Andrew's Street, map F6
Barclays, Market Hill, map D4;
Barclays, Bene't Street, map D5;
Barclays, Sidney Street, map E3
HSBC, Market Hill, map D4
Lloyds TSB, Regent Street;
Lloyds TSB, St Andrew's Street, map F6;
Lloyds TSB, Sidney Street, map E4
NatWest, Bene't Street, map D5

## MAIN POST OFFICE

Main post office is in St Andrew's Street; map E4

## SPORT

The Abbey Swimming Pool, Whitehill Road; Tel: 01223 213352
Cambridge Parkside Pools, Gonville Place; Tel: 01223 446104
Kelsey Kerridge Sports Hall, Queen Anne Terrace; Tel: 01223 462226

## EMERGENCIES
**Fire, ambulance or police**
Tel: 999

**Cambridge Police Station**
Parkside
Tel: 01223 358966

**Addenbrooke's Hospital**
Hills Road has an accident and emergency department
Tel: 01223 217118

**24-hour petrol station**
Sainsbury's, Coldhams Lane

**24-hour breakdown service**
Tunbridge Lane Motors, Tunbridge Lane, Bottisham
Tel: 01223 811849

# INDEX

# CITY-BREAK GUIDES

These full-colour guides come with stunning new photography capturing the special essence of some of Britain's loveliest cities. Each is divided into easy-reference sections where you will find something for everyone – from walk maps to fabulous shopping, from sightseeing highlights to keeping the kids entertained, from recommended restaurants to tours and trips ... and much, much more.

## BATH

Stylish and sophisticated – just two adjectives that sum up the delightful Roman city of Bath, which saw a resurgence of popularity in Georgian times and in the 21st century is once again a vibrant and exciting place to be.

## CAMBRIDGE

Historic architecture mingles with hi-tech revolution in the university city of Cambridge, where stunning skylines over surrounding fenland meet the style and sophistication of modern city living.

## CHESTER

Savour the historic delights of the Roman walls and charming black-and-white architecture, blending seamlessly with the contemporary shopping experience that make Chester such an exhilarating city.

## OXFORD

City and university life intertwine in Oxford, with its museums, bookstores and all manner of sophisticated entertainment to entice visitors to its hidden alleyways, splendid quadrangles and skyline of dreaming spires.

## STRATFORD

Universally appealing, the picturesque streets of Stratford draw visitors back time and again to explore Shakespeare's birthplace, but also to relish the theatres and stylish riverside town that exists today.

## YORK

A warm northern welcome and modern-day world-class shops and restaurants await you in York, along with its ancient city walls, Viking connections and magnificent medieval Minster rising above the rooftops.

Jarrold Publishing, Healey House, Dene Road, Andover, Hampshire, SP10 2AA, UK

**Sales: 01264 409206**
**Enquiries: 01264 409200**
**Fax: 01264 334110**
e-mail: heritagesales@jarrold-publishing.co.uk
website: www.britguides.com

## MAIN ROUTES IN AND OUT OF CAMBRIDGE

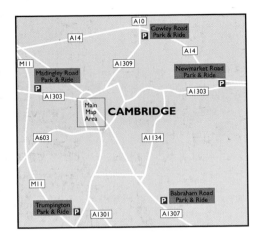

## Park and ride services leave regularly for central Cambridge from:

**Cowley Road Park and Ride**
On the A1309

**Newmarket Park and Ride**
On the A1303

**Babraham Road Park and Ride**
On the A1307

**Trumpington Road Park and Ride**
At junction 11 of the M11

**Madingley Road Park and Ride**
At junction 13 of the M11

See page 95 for further details